Coming Out to Parents

Coming Out to Parents

A Two-way Survival Guide for Lesbians and Gay Men and Their Parents

Mary V. Borhek

THE PILGRIM PRESS • CLEVELAND, OHIO

The Pilgrim Press, Cleveland 44115
Copyright © 1983 Mary V. Borhek
All rights reserved. Published 1983

Printed in the United States of America
6th printing, 1991

Library of Congress Cataloging in Publication Data

Borhek, Mary V., 1922-
  Coming out to parents.

  Bibliography: p. 203
  1. Lesbians—Family relationships.   2. Homosexuals,
Male—Family relationships.   3. Parent and child.
4. Adult children.   I. Title.
HQ75.5B68   1983   646.7'8   83-3971
ISBN 0-8298-0665-2 (pbk.)

To my children—
Emily, Barbara, and Eric—
and to Hans and Brian,
who have become part of
the family circle

Contents

Introduction: A Two-way Mirror

It would be impossible to deal, in one book, with all the specialized situations in which lesbians and gay men come out to their parents. For example, certain ethnic and racial backgrounds pose particular problems; other cultural circumstances also make coming out more difficult. I have written mainly out of my own experience and the experiences of those with whom I have come in contact.

In writing this book I have had difficulties with terminology. At present there are no terms related to sexual orientation that please everybody. Homosexuality is a clinical term many gay men find offensive; many lesbians feel the term applies only to men, not to women. Gay, which used to apply to men and women, now applies, in most geographical areas, only to men and should be used as an adjective, not as a noun. Some want it to be capitalized—Gay—and others are satisfied to let it be spelled with a lower-case *g*. Women prefer to be referred to as lesbians.

To avoid using the words homosexuality and homosexual in most of the book, I have used same-sex orientation and same-sex-oriented. Again, these are not satisfactory choices to some people, because they sound too clinical and seem to ignore the affectional aspect of the orientation.

The word orientation itself is not wholly satisfactory, because it implies that a person can be oriented or adjusted in a particular sexual direction. It is preferable, however, to the words sexual preference, which indicate to some people that a man or woman has made a conscious choice that he relates lovingly and sexually to men rather than to women or that she relates lovingly and sexually to women rather than to men.

The authors of the book *Sexual Preference* deal with the erroneous meaning of this term.

> Although we have entitled our present work *Sexual Preference,* we do not mean to imply that a given sexual orientation is the result of a conscious decision or is as changeable as the many moment-by-moment decisions we make in our lives. Neither homosexuals nor heterosexuals are what they are by design. . . . There is no reason to think it would be any easier for homosexual men or women to reverse their sexual orientation than it would be for heterosexual readers to become predominantly or exclusively homosexual.[1]

A paper prepared for study and discussion at a 1979 conference in Milwaukee for Lutheran campus ministers states: "We are using 'sexual orientation' here in its broadest reference to our sensations and perceptions of ourselves in relation to others, in terms of not only interpersonal attraction but also such 'non-sexual' enterprises as achieving success, child-rearing, etc."

I have written this book as a two-way mirror for both the same-sex-oriented person and her or his parents. I hope daughter or son and mother and father will want to read all the chapters. (Chapter 9, "Religious Issues and a Same-sex Orientation," has been included for parents for whom religion is an issue in their difficulties with their child's orientation.) This way the adult child can gain some understanding of the parents' perspectives and of her or his own adjustment to life. The parent who reads the book will gain a perspective of his or her own life situation as well as that of the same-sex-oriented daughter or son. Thus both sides can come to understand why the child's sexual orientation may seem so shocking, can come to understand the changes and upheavals going on within the parents, so each side can begin coping constructively with the new situation.

Generally, the chapters are best read in sequence, but chapter 9, which deals with religious issues, may be read at any point. Parents who are having problems with the religious aspect of a same-sex orientation particularly may want to turn to this chapter first.

I am sad that such elaborate preparation is necessary in order for a gay or lesbian child to be open with his or her parents about the person the child really is. Society through the centuries—largely because of a lack of genuine information—has laid a cruel burden on the same-sex-oriented person. Only now is the world at large beginning to deal more realistically and less hurtfully with this orientation.

I dream of a time when parents can realize without anguish that their son is gay or their daughter lesbian, because society will have learned that a same-sex orientation is not sick, dangerous, or evil. What a person, whether heterosexual or homosexual, *does* with his or her sexuality may indeed be evil, sick, or dangerous, but in either case the orientation itself is not.

What if there were no persecution of lesbian and gay persons, no fear in being one's total self, and no agonized coming out to oneself, to one's parents, to others? Obviously, society has not yet incorporated this vision. Many battles are still to be fought before there can be mutual understanding, mutual respect, and mutual acceptance between heterosexual and same-sex-oriented persons.

As a gay or lesbian child, in coming out to your parents and in helping them deal with your sexual orientation you are taking a step in the direction of mutuality. If you as parents make an effort to come to terms with your child's sexuality, you also are moving in a constructive direction.

Some people do not consider this movement constructive. To them, these ideas are destructive of all the values they hold dearest. If you are one of these people, please do not throw this book aside in fear, anger, and disgust. Its real purpose is not to present a theory of sexual and social evolution that may or may not come to pass. Rather, it is designed to help you deal with a difficult fact in your life; much information in these pages can help you do this.

Whatever your ideas about a same-sex orientation, you are being forced to cope with the information that your child is lesbian or gay. You can cut off contact or communication with your child, but this will not change her or his sexual orientation, *because she or he cannot and should not change in the way that you want*—should not because this would violate the person your child really is. How much better to maintain contact with your child and give yourself time to learn more about yourself, your child, and the situation in which you find yourself.

Although my name appears as author of this book, the book could not have come into being without the assistance—sometimes substantial—of many people. Some can be named; others prefer to remain anonymous or be referred to by fictitious names.

Douglas Elwood, John Grace, Jennifer Feigal, Sylvia Rudolph, and Rabbi Moshe Adler gave much help in various capacities. My children by birth or by relationship with a family member, as well as many lesbians and gay men—and in some cases their families—have also provided a great deal of assistance.

I am particularly indebted to Pearl P. Rosenberg, Ph.D.,

assistant dean of admissions and student affairs of the University of Minnesota Medical School, who, in 1978, addressed the second annual workshop sponsored in Minneapolis by Families of Gays and Lesbians in cooperation with the Neighborhood Counseling Center. She was the first person to point out to me, as part of the workshop group, that parents go through a grieving process when a lesbian or gay child comes out to them. From this beginning I put together a talk I used for a number of lesbian/gay groups, which ultimately developed into this book.

Those who find this book helpful do so because of the persons I have mentioned. The pain a family experiences when it learns one of its members is same-sex-oriented may be lessened because of the willingness of these people to share their stories or serve as advisers.

For any parent reading this book the journey ahead may not be easy, but life was not designed to be easy—exciting, difficult, depressing, monotonous, joyous, but almost never easy.

Coming Out to Parents

Chapter 1

So You Want to Come Out to Your Parents

So you want to come out to your parents. You want to tell them an important fact about yourself of which, in all probability, they are unaware: If you are a woman, you want to tell them you are a lesbian; if you are a man, you want to tell them you are gay.

Or you have already come out to them, and the ensuing explosion has left you angry, alienated, wounded, and bitter.

Or you have told your parents, and they have not referred to the matter since. It is as if you had not said anything.

Or they want you to talk with their minister, priest, or rabbi. Or they want you to seek counseling. (Obviously, they hope you can change.)

Or they keep handing you literature published by ex-gay organizations—groups (usually with a strong religious orientation) that promise help in changing from a same-sex orientation to a heterosexual orientation or support in living a celibate life-style.

Or they let you know, not too subtly, that *you* are welcome at home, but your friend is not.

Or possibly they have let you know, quickly and definitely, that you are no longer their daughter or son.

Your parents' reactions to the news that their child is same-sex-oriented are likely to be emotional and, unfortunately, negative. Why must it be like this, you wonder. Why can they not be loving and accepting of this aspect of yourself? It may have been hard for you yourself to accept your sexual orientation. If they could receive your information with at least a measure of equanimity, it would be much easier for you. When they seem greatly disturbed, you are forced to retrace all the agonizing steps you have taken, as you wait for them to work through their difficulties with your gayness or lesbianism.

If you want to help them deal with what you are going to tell them—or have already told them—you need some understanding of the social and sexual climate in which your parents matured. Until the late 1960s your parents never saw the word homosexuality in magazines or newspapers—at least not the ones most people read. The word appeared in dictionaries, in some encyclopedias, in scholarly publications, and in books that wanted to be slightly daring. Homosexuality was not a topic of general social conversation, although there were plenty of crude jokes about fairies, homos, queers, dykes, amazons, and lezzies. As for the church, homosexuality was not mentioned from the pulpit or discussed at church meetings. It was hardly even breathed at counseling sessions in the privacy of the pastor's study, and almost never did it find its way into the confessional.

Until I was seventeen I had never heard the word homosexual. I came across it as I was reading a rather unorthodox book that had been recommended to me by a self-consciously iconoclastic young friend. When I looked up the word in the dictionary I was shocked. The definition was restrained, as definitions in dictionaries are apt to be, and was taken care of in one brief phrase: "n., eroticism for one of the same sex."

I was confused. I had been led to believe that such feelings could happen only between men and women, not between persons of the same sex. How was it possible for a man to have sexual feelings for another man or a woman for another woman?

For some time I mulled over this information. Apparently, persons of the same sex could become sexually excited about each other. I did not understand how this was possible. Nor did I realize that feelings of genuine love could accompany the sexual feelings.

During my first year of college I was confronted with what appeared to be too intimate a relationship between two young women in my circle of friends. The rest of the group frequently discussed the situation when the two women were not present. I cannot remember anyone ever saying the word lesbian—if indeed we even knew the word. No one ever verbalized why we were concerned about the situation or what we thought was actually going on when the two women were together in one or the other's room, with the door closed. We just knew this kind of thing was not done.

We never learned whether our suspicions were correct. Neither woman returned the following year. One transferred to a college near her family's new home; the other married her steady boyfriend during the summer.

As I moved into adulthood I discovered that there might be unpleasant consequences to being homosexual. Because at that time homosexuality was considered a crime and a sin rather than an orientation toward life, it was not surprising that persons who were homosexual were subject to blackmail, that they could face professional and social ruin if their homosexuality were discovered, or that they could even be jailed. No one questioned *why* homosexuality was a crime. The law said it was, and no one was motivated to argue with the law. If people chose to be perverse, they had to suffer the penalty.

This is the climate in which most parents grew up. People did not know much about homosexuality and saw no reason to learn more. If you, a lesbian or gay person, were born in the 1950s or 1960s, you probably cannot entirely understand the feelings with which your parents may have to struggle, because the social climate has changed significantly in the past twelve to fifteen years. Your parents are laboring under a whole body of unconscious assumptions, most likely never even specifically formulated, gathered from a word here, an innuendo there, a significant silence, a whispered remark. Most parents do not know why they think about homosexuality in the way they do or from what sources they have inherited their ideas.

This kind of unconscious "information" is the hardest to deal with or change. Straight people never thought to question their ideas about homosexuality. They "knew" certain things about it and none of these things was good.

In addition to your understanding something of the climate in which your parents grew up, it will be helpful for you to see your parents as persons rather than as father and mother. Now that you are an adult, your parents are no longer responsible for raising, disciplining, and training you. For you to relate to them in the former parent/child ways is no longer helpful or desirable. You need to see them and relate to them as adult to adult. (If you have not yet attained legal majority, the situation is different.)

Separating the real personhood of a parent from her or his parental role is not always easy. Attitudes and habits formed over the first fifteen to twenty years of one's life are hard to change. An adult child often slips back unconsciously into former patterns of relationship with his or her parents, and the parents often deal with their grown-up child in parental rather than adult ways. Outwardly, parents and child are adults, but inwardly, the adult daughter or son may retain a vague sense of being the little girl or boy relating to the grown-up persons who for many years held the reins of power and who seemed to be so much wiser and more competent than the child. The parents also find it hard to remember that this person, their child, who for years needed guidance and discipline, no longer requires this type of care. Not to slip back at least slightly into old habits of relating to each other is difficult for parents and grown child.

In addition, try to gain a perspective on the problems your parents are facing at this particular time in their lives. What are the pressures they may be feeling? Are they dealing with thwarted dreams of career or status? Are they coming face to face with the inevitability of aging and consequent mortality? Are they having problems with *their* parents? Are they also being confronted by difficulties with other children in your family? The more you can see your parents as two individuals struggling with their own issues of personhood as well as with the demands of the older and younger generations of the family, the better you will understand their reactions to your coming out to them.

Although you may have some trouble visualizing it, once upon a time—perhaps not so long ago—your parents were young. Life stretched before them with wonderful and seemingly endless possibilities. In those days their chins were firmer and single, their hips narrower, their stomachs flatter, their hair one color, and their muscles did not feel like tired rubber bands. Now, even though they may look youthful, with each passing day they realize that life is not the same as it used to be.

Twenty to thirty years ago they had hopes and dreams and goals. They could be whatever they wanted to be, accomplish whatever they set themselves to accomplish. Opportunity beckoned; the future was bright, the horizon almost limitless.

Your parents may be realizing gradually that many of these marvelous dreams will never be fulfilled. Somehow they have slipped into certain patterns, and the difficulty and pain of altering these patterns may be more than they care to undertake. All of us live with a psychological as well as a physical law of inertia that makes it easier to remain in a known routine—even though it may be uncomfortable—than to change course and take a new direction. Leaving the safety of the known for the risk of the unknown can be frightening.

With each passing year your parents may be increasingly aware of their unfulfilled dreams, their mistaken decisions and choices in the past, the things they have not done that now may never be accomplished. They begin to realize that while they used to be able to keep going strong until 1 A.M., now they begin to wilt at 10 or 11 P.M. They find their eyes at half-mast over the evening paper. They fall asleep watching television. The french fried onion rings they used to be able to eat by the basketful now cause indigestion, and feet that never hurt before start aching. The signs are there: *I am getting old.*

They do not *say* that to themselves. They joke about the little aches and pains, about going to sleep over the newspaper or while watching television. But underneath, well concealed from others and perhaps partially hidden from themselves, uneasiness and frustration due to these creeping limitations may be building. At times they may experience a touch of panic: "What will become of me?"

They may not be conscious of these thoughts. All they know is they feel vaguely unhappy or slightly depressed, as if the sun that had shone so brightly had retreated behind a cloud.

Other pressures are also common to most parents in the

middle or later years. They want life to be better for their children than it was for them. This in itself is natural and commendable. The problem arises when the parents discover that their idea of better may not coincide with the adult son's or daughter's idea of better. It may be difficult—or even impossible—for the parents to understand how a particular course of action or a philosophy of life can be satisfying to their child when it is so unpalatable to them.

Whether they are aware of it or not, most parents have an instinctive sense that their children are their—the parents'—second chance at life. Usually, such parents are sophisticated enough to realize they cannot push their children into a particular profession or vocation in order to satisfy their own unfulfilled dreams. Still, they want their children to be richer and smarter and better and wiser—and possibly happier—than they have been.

This wish is not a totally unselfish one. Although your parents want you to do well in life for your own sake, they also need you to do well so they can prove to themselves that they are not failures as parents.

In addition, children provide continuity into the future for the parents, who may not be conscious of this feeling. Those who believe in life after death feel they do not need grandchildren and great-grandchildren to achieve immortality. And yet . . . and yet . . . despite all one's rational knowledge and belief, a visceral kind of yearning wants one's genes, one's name, one's bloodline carried on into the future.

Then comes the child's announcement, "I am lesbian" or "I am gay." One brief sentence strikes at the heart of all the unconscious hopes and dreams and wishes with which the parents have surrounded their child. Can you understand why such an announcement arouses deep feelings within parents?

Another aspect of your parents' lives may be affected by

your announcement of your sexual orientation. Although they may never have talked about this with you (in all likelihood they have not), there was probably a time when their sex life was fairly intense. And now? Like many other things at this time in their lives, their sexual energy may be scaling down also.

Your announcement that you are lesbian or gay, relating as it does to your sexual nature, could be upsetting, because it touches the area that may be most sensitive to your parents. Because sexual drives are connected with some of the deepest instincts of the human race, sex is never impersonal. No one can approach the subject neutrally. The fact that we are male or female, the unspoken sexual messages as well as the spoken ones (if any) when we were children, the accumulation of our sexual experience or lack of it—all these influence each of us so that it is impossible to deal with sexual matters from a wholly neutral standpoint.

In addition, it is often difficult for parents to face the fact that their children are sexual beings. Generally, parents expect their children, as they grow up, to begin dating and eventually become engaged, to marry and in time have children. Parents know their children are sexual persons, but the sexual development parents visualize takes place within the forms prescribed by society. Sexuality that manifests itself in the standard heterosexual mode— dating, marriage, children—is not nearly as threatening or upsetting as sexuality that departs from this pattern.

In telling your parents you are lesbian or gay you are telling them you are indeed a sexual being, but that your sexuality is not channeled into the ordered patterns that are safe and familiar. Suddenly, you are a stranger. The sexual fears, prohibitions, and taboos that have been bred into your parents throughout their lives are activated by your information. You, their child, belong to the forces that are trying to undermine the traditional values of home and family life. The sexual revolution has been brought home to them in a personal, unmistakable, upsetting way. It would hardly be surprising, then, if your parents go into a tailspin.

As One Parent to Another

So far in this chapter I have addressed same-sex-oriented children. I am shifting now and speaking as one parent to other parents.

Earlier in this chapter you may have read much with which you could identify. Or you may have felt that what was stated did not touch you, that nothing bore much relation to your life. You may even have felt some resistance: "This isn't how it was or is for me." Perhaps you are right.

But sometimes it is difficult for us to see what is closest at hand, *because we do not choose to.* I am not speaking of a conscious, rational choice that lines up the facts, pro and con, and from this information makes a decision. I am speaking of choices made because our unconscious psychic antennae warn us that these facts will make us uncomfortable. And so we do not allow ourselves to be aware of such facts or situations. We never admit them to our conscious minds.

To face the facts of our middle and later years, especially in today's youth-oriented culture, is not easy. We do not want to deal with the human ambivalence that wants "the best" for our children both because we want our children to be happy and because we want them to bring credit to us. Often we do the right thing, not for the wrong reasons, but for both the right *and* the wrong reasons. Mostly, *we do not want to probe into the matter of sexuality—ours or our children's.* We were raised in a simpler age, when we knew which kind of sexual behavior was accepted and which was taboo. Now our children are asking us to make major revisions in our thinking, feeling, perceiving—our understanding of being. More than this, our children are asking us to go against inherited information accepted for centuries as truth.

I have found it illuminating to discover the roots in antiquity of many of the erroneous beliefs about homosexuality that are still generally accepted as fact. A hundred years' worth of emerging scientific information about homosexuality has made only a dent in the popular understanding of a same-sex orientation.

Although you may not believe it now, your child's coming out to you can be a vehicle for greater self-understanding and deeper relationships with others. "The experience of change, . . . of being on unfamiliar ground, of doing things differently is frightening. It always was and always will be," M. Scott Peck has written in *The Road Less Traveled*. And yet, he says, "it is in this whole process of meeting and solving problems that life has its meaning."[1]

Unquestionably, as the parents of a lesbian or gay child, you have been presented with a real challenge—but also with a real opportunity for growth in your life. You may not welcome this opportunity, but often we do not welcome those situations that strip us of our comfortable insulation, that force us to leave our secure cocoon and venture forth into new and unchosen territory.

Chapter 2

The Big Decision

If you are a gay man or a lesbian who has not yet come out to your parents, you may be apprehensive or downright scared. You do not know how to tell your parents so the pain—for them and for you—will be minimal. Is it best to tell them in person? If a continent lies between where you live and where they live, should you write them a letter or call them on the phone? Or should you wait until you and your parents are together?

You have constructed a hundred different scenarios about your telling them and every one is bad. Avoiding such things as tears, anger, and pain seems impossible. Or you visualize the worst: "You are no longer our daughter (son)."

You wish the scenario could go something like this: "We're glad you've told us. This information doesn't change our feelings for you, except perhaps to make us love you even more because we realize you went through some tough times by yourself when you discovered you are lesbian (gay)." It is unlikely your coming out will be received in quite this manner. You are hoping for an immediate reaction that, realistically, may take months or years to achieve.

How can you tell your parents so they will not react negatively? Unfortunately, the answer to this question is that there is no way you can be sure how your parents will react. They may seem to hold liberal beliefs. Yet when they are confronted with your alternative sexual orientation, they may react with surprising intolerance. Anyone who has seen the Katharine Hepburn/Spencer Tracy movie *Guess Who's Coming to Dinner* has had a glimpse of the discrepancy between what people say they believe and how they feel and react when the reality confronts them.

Other parents, when they learn of their children's same-sex orientation, may draw on reserves of strength and love they were not aware they had. I remember the scene in the television movie *Sergeant Matlovich vs. the U.S. Air Force* in which Matlovich and his father face each other for the first time after the father has learned that his son is gay. He is angry with his son, not because Leonard is gay, but because he has not allowed his father to share the pain through which he had gone in learning to face and deal with his sexual orientation. This is not the reaction Sergeant Matlovich had expected from his father.

In my own case, when I was confronted with the fact that my son, Eric, is gay, I reacted in a way no one could have foreseen. Because I had already lost one member of the family—my husband, through divorce—I dared not let the family shrink further. Even though Eric was gay, which I (at that point) totally condemned, I needed him as a continuing member of the family. Eventually, I moved far beyond this simplistic attitude of condemnation to understanding and acceptance of a same-sex orientation, as I have described in *My Son Eric*.[1]

As you can see, parental reactions are not predictable. Your parents may react in ways you cannot foresee. Perhaps, however, when you tell your parents of your sexual orientation, your worst fears will be realized. As you decide whether or not to come out to them, you need to face up to this possibility but not let it lead you to conclude that you should not tell them about your sexual orientation. It could help you assess more realistically what you are asking of your parents and realize that changing attitudes on this scale takes time, that you will need love and patience as they struggle to replace their former ideas with new information and comprehension.

There are a lot of good reasons why you may want to come out to your parents. Pretending to them, year after year, that you are someone you are not is hard. If your parents do not know the totality that is you, including your lesbianism or gayness, an invisible barrier exists between you and them.

You have to watch carefully everything you say so you do not let slip some piece of information that might give away your secret. "After we've talked about the weather and my job, I have nothing more to say to my parents, because all my leisure activities take place in the gay community and they don't know I'm gay," one young man said, in a discussion about coming out to parents. His problem is not unusual in the gay or lesbian community. If your parents do not know of your sexual orientation, a growing sense of estrangement is apt to develop between your family and you because you are not being yourself with them. You are always playing a role.

Sometimes specific events provide good reasons for coming out to your parents. For instance, self-disclosure becomes rather urgent if you are a visible lesbian or gay activist. If there is a chance that your picture or a statement you make may be printed in a newspaper—any newspaper—it would be better for you to tell your parents about yourself, rather than having them learn the truth from a clipping sent to them by a friend or acquaintance. Do not assume this could not happen, even though you may be living in California and your parents are in Maine. The world is shrinking, news can travel in the most unexpected ways.

A visit by your parents to the town or city where you live might also cause you to give serious thought to coming out to them. More than one lesbian or gay couple has had to set up elaborate subterfuges when parents come to visit if the parents have no idea of the true state of affairs. Either the couple has to pretend they are friends sharing living quarters (and you better have two bedrooms, each with a bed in it) or the lover has to move everything out of the house or apartment for the length of the visit. During the parents' stay there is continual fear that some telltale evidence has been overlooked and not removed. ("Have I hidden my gay/lesbian books and magazines well enough so my parents will not stumble on them? Is there something that might reveal the truth, some sign to which I have become so accustomed that I am no longer aware of it?")

Often the psychic cost of concealing from your parents the information that you are same-sex-oriented is high. You are implicitly denying the worth of your true self and the worth of your relationship with your lover. You are living out the idea that a same-sex-oriented person *is* a second-class citizen and family member and that the relationship with a lover really *is* inferior to the relationship between married partners. This kind of self-disparagement is so subtle you may not realize that it *is* disparaging.

But the most difficult task you face may be coming out to your parents. A thousand unconscious ties, beginning at the moment of birth and perhaps before, bind us compulsively to our parents. In the case of adoptive parents, the ties may be slightly different but possibly even more compulsive because of the lack of a biologic bond.

Augustus Y. Napier, a psychologist specializing in family therapy, has caught the essence of the adult child's dilemma in *The Family Crucible*, when he writes about "the power of the primordial parent, the source of all oppression and of final deliverance."[2] This is what our parents represented to us when we were helpless babies. At that age we had no words with which to frame our conclusions. Nevertheless, the idea is indelibly entered in our internal mental and emotional "computers." It is one of the unconscious components of our lives—and I am referring to every human being, not only lesbian and gay persons. We can deal with these compulsive bonds only by bringing them into consciousness, at the cost of greater or lesser emotional pain, after which we can begin to deal with them on a maturer level.

Coming out to your parents is usually a highly emotional issue. It cannot be resolved on a purely rational level because of the deep, unconscious emotional bonds as well as the unconscious awareness of your family's rules, those unstated guidelines to the way your particular family deals with life in all its varied aspects, guidelines you absorb seemingly by osmosis.

If you have a lover, the issue is complicated by your need to give the relationship importance and your need for your lover to be part of the family. Any decision—whether to tell or not to tell—carries risks to the familial relationship and to the lover relationship.

The reasons you choose not to tell your parents may be overriding. If one or both of them are old or have serious health problems that might be aggravated by your information or if you feel there is a strong possibility they may disown you, you may choose to say nothing. A more likely result you may envision is that your parents will never be able to come to terms with your information, and you therefore do not want to subject them or yourself to a never-ending tug-of-war.

Perhaps you feel no need to tell your parents. This may

be a psychologically sound decision for you, based on realistic wrestling with the issue. But Don Clark, a gay therapist and author of *Loving Someone Gay*, warns that if in your imagination you find yourself again and again telling a particular person you are lesbian/gay, you had better tell that person about your sexual orientation. You are using too much precious emotional energy to maintain your secret. Similarly, he says, if you have to go to some effort to hide your same-sex orientation from a specific person, "you must, for your own survival, tell him or her sooner or later."[3]

If you do decide to come out, are you going to tell only one parent or both? If your parents are divorced, telling only one parent presents no particular problem. Be sure, however, that the parent who has been told knows that the other parent has not. Otherwise you may be setting up a sticky situation for yourself.

If your parents are not divorced but you feel inclined to confide in one and not the other, there may be some family dynamics in action to which you have not heretofore given much thought. You have not analyzed *why* it is always easier to talk with Mom than with Dad or vice versa. It is a fact of life that she (he) seems to understand you better or is not as likely to get upset as the other parent.

Much more is involved in this situation than is apparent at first. Some elements may have to do with whether one parent treats you more as an adult whereas the other still sees you, at least to some extent, as a child. More likely these reflect the pattern of interaction between your parents, and your decision to tell one parent and not the other follows lines of communication and action that your parents have established unconsciously as the family's way of living together.

As an adult, you need not follow the prevailing family pattern. If you do choose to follow it, it might help your own self-understanding to be aware of why you are choosing to tell one parent only. Obviously, you are choosing not to tell one of your parents because you envision an uncomfortable conflict over your sexual orientation. You may have to balance your desire to avoid such discomfort against the fact that you may be putting a strain on the parent you tell by asking that parent to keep the information secret from her or his partner. You are forming an alliance with one parent against the other. Almost certainly this is not a new alliance, but further evidence of a rift that has existed between your parents—as well as between yourself and one parent—for a considerable period. If there is such an emotional split between your parents, telling both of them may mean they are polarized even more as one feels the need to defend you to the other.

There are no easy answers to such a dilemma, but I think you, as a son or daughter of such parents, need to recognize *you are not and never have been* the cause of the division between your parents. The relationship probably has a flaw that can be traced back to its beginning.

The issue is too complex to discuss in detail here, but some exploration of your family relationships might help you make your decision. Reading one or more books dealing with family dynamics (several are listed at the end of this book) will give you some insight into the unconscious rules in your family as well as into your own feelings and your relationships within your family. *The Family Crucible* in particular clearly shows the actual dynamics of family "triangulation" (chapters 12, 13, 14).[4] If counseling is available and you feel the need to examine your family system with someone who can help you gain insights, it might be wise to seek this outside help.

Before you decide whether to tell or not to tell your parents you are lesbian or gay, the matter is worthy of your best research and effort, even though this may require a considerable investment of time and energy and perhaps money.

Whether the outcome of your revelation—should you decide to make it—is good (your parents accept and continue to love you) or bad (they never do come to terms with your information), the experience will not have been wasted. Your action may have been painful and, from your point of view, may seem to have been unsuccessful (your parents did not provide the approval/understanding/acceptance you desired). Yet if you emerge from the process with a greater understanding of yourself and of the dynamics of person-to-person and family interaction, you will have been rewarded for whatever time, work, emotion, and money you put into the effort. Self-knowledge and self-understanding usually do not come easy.

Possibly, by being honest with your parents about your real self you are giving them an opportunity to grow. The results may be far better than you can imagine. In time—and I want to emphasize this—*in time* you may be closer to your parents and family because you risked entrusting them with the knowledge of who you really are. You may have a clearer sense of your own identity and a new sense of freedom and self-respect because now you are not hiding your real self. You may have a new sense of yourself as a responsible adult because you have dealt straightforwardly with a difficult issue. You may have a clearer understanding of yourself in your intimate relationships—those with family, lover, and close friends. You may now be able to share joyfully and with a sense of well-being with the significant persons in your life because you have taken the positive step of being real with them.

In other words, by risking coming out to your parents you have given yourself and them an opportunity to grow.

Chapter 3

Grief Often Does Not Look Like Grief

"How could you do this to us?"

This question is one of the commoner reactions of parents to the news that they have a lesbian daughter or a gay son. Sometimes it is asked in anguish, sometimes in anger.

Some parents ask themselves a companion question: "Where did we go wrong?"

Neither query is asked in order to receive objective information. Both are reflexive, knee-jerk reactions to sudden shock and pain.

Undoubtedly, many thoughts and feelings are going through your parents' heads. If it were possible to get a slow-motion reading of these thoughts and feelings, it would probably include shock, confusion, pain, anger, guilt, and a desire to get rid of some of the guilt by shifting the blame.

You have challenged some sensitive traditional beliefs your parents hold. Any challenge to convention is likely at first to provoke bewildered resentment.[1] In addition, your parents are apt to feel tremendous guilt. Anything that happens to their child is *their fault*. They have failed. They must have been bad parents. Their child is gay or lesbian because of what they have done or left undone. Instinctively, they voice a question in order to shift some of the heavy guilt that has descended on them: *"How could you do this to us?"* If your parents have not been afraid to be angry with you, they may ask the question in anger. If they feel that *good* parents do not get angry, they may ask the question with anguished tears in their eyes. Either way the question can be devastating to you. (But then your information has been devastating to your parents.)

The disclosure that you are lesbian or gay has set in motion grief reactions within your parents. And chances are they have not the slightest idea they are experiencing grief. In fact, this may surprise you and your parents. After all, you are alive and in good health. Why should your parents grieve?

Ira J. Tanner, in his book *Healing the Pain of Everyday Loss*, lists different types of losses.[2] The death of a loved one, divorce, and loss of one's job are not the only causes of grief. Moving to a new house; the death of a favorite pet, plant, or tree; job promotion (surprisingly); loss of family heirlooms; seasonal loss, such as the passing of summer, fall, Christmas—all these can cause grief reactions of varying intensity.

But you are alive and healthy, so what have your parents lost?

They have lost an image of you, an idea about you, the identification of you as a heterosexual person. From the moment of your birth they have been creating and adding to a mental picture of who you are. As you have grown and developed they have added details. One assumption about you they probably have never questioned. Most likely they assumed you were heterosexually oriented and that you would someday marry, settle down, and raise a family, like they did.

Now this fundamental assumption about you has been demolished. Your parents discover that they do not know as much about you as they thought. They have been deceived!

They *have* been deceived but not with malicious intent. In large measure they have deceived themselves by making an assumption they never thought to verify. In addition, you *have* deceived them by letting them continue to assume you are straight. You may have actively encouraged them to think this by various means. Often lesbian and gay young people lie and make omissions about who they are seeing, when, how. Dating is generally the alibi used to conceal lesbian or gay relationships. Such young persons invent names, places, and what happened on these dates in order to hide the truth they are not ready to disclose to their parents, because disclosure could blow the young persons' precarious world to pieces. Probably, these young persons who are becoming aware of their different sexual orientation are struggling with at least some self-loathing; after all, society has graphically told the lesbians and gay men how sick, sinful, despised, and repulsive they are. Whatever deception you have engaged in has been undertaken as a means of self-preservation, not consciously to defraud or wound your parents.

Besides other losses your parents are experiencing, they are experiencing a loss of faith in one of their fundamental beliefs, that *of course everyone is born heterosexual unless they are sick, neurotic, rebellious, or perverse.* Your parents are therefore grappling with a double grief: the loss of the *you* they thought they knew in every aspect of your being and the loss of a basic tenet, that everyone is born heterosexual and deviates from this only because of calamity or willful perversity. Of course your parents are experiencing loss. Of course they will need to grieve.

Related to their primary loss are allied sources of pain. For instance, they may feel you have forsaken their value system. Almost certainly your parents had hoped you would help perpetuate the things they have valued in their lives: the establishment of a home and family, the value of monogamy (even if they are divorced, they may still believe in one-at-a-time monogamous commitments), and if they are religiously inclined, the upholding of their beliefs about sin and righteousness. Your new and unfamiliar sexual attitudes may threaten to cast them adrift from familiar moorings.

Although they may not realize it at first, perhaps they see this conflict between value systems as a personal defeat. Is it not up to the parents to shape their child's values, to pass on to the coming generation the beliefs and attitudes they deem important and necessary for a full and moral life? Somewhere along the way, they believe, they have failed to transmit to you the ideas they value. Suddenly, insidiously, their own child is the enemy. They are suffering defeat and loss at the hands of their child.

They may also see your apparent forsaking of their values as a loss of power over their child's life. Or they may interpret this supposed loss of power as a rejection of themselves. Unconsciously, most parents mistakenly believe that if their children really honor and love them, the children will adhere closely to their parents' values.

Another grief your parents may be experiencing concerns their loss of expectation of a son- or daughter-in-law. There will be no beautiful wedding to which they can invite relatives and friends, none of the excitement that surrounds such an event, no showers and gifts. Before you dismiss this loss as shallow and trivial, remember that these are deeply ingrained cultural patterns that have their roots in the establishment of a protective environment where children may be created and nurtured.

In addition, your parents may be grieving the loss of potential grandchildren you might have given them. If you have already been married and have had children, in all likelihood you and your mate are getting or have gotten a divorce, and this, too, grieves your parents.

Clearly, both you and your parents need to be aware that they will experience some psychic losses when you tell them of your lesbian or gay orientation. Because these losses are real, it is important that your parents grieve—and that you should be willing for them to do so.

Many gay or lesbian persons I talk with tell me the same thing: "I have told my parents, but they aren't dealing with it at all. I've given them books to read, but they won't read them. We never talk about it." I can hear the hurt in their voices, because their parents seem to be denying the very personhood of their daughter or son.

Denial is a common way of expressing one's grief. What the parents are denying, however, is not the personhood of their child; they are denying to themselves this one fact about their child because they are unwilling or unable to face it and deal with it. And, of course, this is the one fact their child wants them to face—and accept.

The odd thing about grief is that often what people do in its throes does not appear as grief, but rather resembles anger, guilt, blaming, bargaining, denial, and depression. Eventually, the result of all this will be—one hopes—acceptance.

These aspects of grief may not be exhibited as well-defined stages. In fact, they probably will not. They are likely to be more or less scrambled together. Anger may be expressed in a relatively straightforward way, or it may be leaked out in blaming. If anger is repressed and given no outlet, it can lead to depression—anger turned inward. Similarly, guilt may be experienced as guilt, or it may be channeled into other aspects, such as blaming, bargaining, or anger. In addition, all these ungrieflike feelings may be experienced again and again, in no discernible sequence.

Anger in the face of grief may seem to be an odd, sometimes even irrational reaction. When we probe beneath the surface, however, we discover the reasons for it. They are connected to the fight side of the physiological fight-or-flight mechanisms by which the body deals with crises. In addition, grieving persons experience discomfort and confusion because their lives have been disrupted, because they have suffered loss of control over the circumstances of their lives. And so they become angry at themselves for losing control, at others who caused the loss of control, and perhaps ultimately at God or fate or whatever caused this disruption of their lives.

Anger may be expressed in a number of ways. It may rush out explosively, for example, as in the classic "How could you *do* this to us?" or it may be expressed by total silence on the subject. How often have you heard someone say, "I was so angry I couldn't even talk about it"? Your parents' silence may indicate denial, or it may stem from a consuming anger at the blow life has dealt them. Unfortunately, they may be localizing this anger on you rather than on the more abstract designation of "life." They may even be angry that life has dealt such a blow to you, their child. Yet they may be unable to recognize that they are angry or know why. One way or the other, they may be denying feelings.

Many times you have probably greeted the announcement of bad news with the words, "Oh no!" or "You're kidding!" This is a manifestation of the wish to deny that a calamity has occurred. Denial serves as an anesthetic in the first flush of grief. It can separate us for a time from pain that is too intense to bear, and by doing this it can help preserve our emotional equilibrium until the time when we can begin to deal with the crisis. Denial functions as a circuit breaker when the emotional circuits become overloaded.

To survive emotionally and continue to function, a person may deny certain information—in this case that their child is lesbian or gay. I remember the parents of a gay man saying at a Families of Gays and Lesbians meeting, "Between meetings we kind of forget that Jack is gay, and we get along fine. Then we see the meeting date on our calendar, and it forces us to remember that Jack is gay. Every month we struggle with the decision of whether to come to the meeting and think about his being gay, which makes us feel bad, or not to go to the meeting and forget about his gayness."

When denial becomes a way of life it is damaging to the one who denies and to those around him or her. The results of denial have been graphically portrayed in the book and film *Ordinary People*.[3] Unable to deal with the death of her older son, Beth Jarrett eventually finds it necessary to flee from her husband and younger son, disrupting their lives as well as her own.

The real problem with prolonged denial is that it is a prison in which one locks oneself, and only the imprisoned person holds the key to the door. Storming the fortress from without is rarely successful. Patient love may eventually bring results, but it is an exceedingly difficult gift to give.

Guilt is another strong, universal component of grief. Even when no cause and effect relationship exists between a person's actions and the cause of grief, the human reaction usually is, "If only I had done this" or "If I hadn't done that, it wouldn't have happened."

In the case of a child's same-sex orientation, most parents are inundated with guilt. In my own case I knew immediately *why* Eric is gay: *It was because of the home in which he had grown up.* A number of years and a good bit of information later I know it was not my husband's or my fault, that the causes of a same-sex orientation are complex. Thousands of factors, many of which are not yet understood, may contribute to a child's sexual orientation, whether hetero- or homosexual. Nevertheless, most parents of gay or lesbian persons ask themselves sometime or another, "Where did we go wrong?"

Where there is guilt, there has to be blame. And so parents blame themselves or you or outside circumstances.

"How could *you* do this to us?"

"If only we hadn't let him play with dolls (let her play football with the boys) this wouldn't have happened."

"Some evil person must have seduced my child."

"If there wasn't so much publicity in the newspapers and on TV about homosexuality, this wouldn't have happened." And so on and on.

Guilt can be lessened by bargaining. "Well, it's all right if—" if you seek counseling, if you will try to change, if you will live a celibate life. Bargaining is an attempt by your parents to reduce the anxiety level produced by guilt.

A variation of bargaining can be redefinition. Although the thought may not even be verbalized, it can take many forms: "He (she) will change"; "She will meet the right man (He will meet the right woman)"; "This is just a phase." Wishful thinking and false hope can encourage such redefinition. Hope can keep people alive, and without hope they would at times die. But hope can also be a tormentor, particularly if it is founded on unsubstantiated claims. Thus, every assertion that someone has changed will torment your parents—and possibly you, if they keep reminding you of these claims and assertions. Such shreds of hope can torture your parents and you for years.

Depression can also be a means of shifting guilt to others. "Look how bad you have made me feel" may be the unconscious message being conveyed. Because the other person does not want to accept the guilt, the temptation is to tell the depressed one to cheer up or snap out of it. Unfortunately, this does no good. It is more helpful to *validate* or confirm the reality of the depression by telling the person he or she is experiencing a natural reaction and that it is probably only temporary. If depression continues or deepens, the depressed person may need professional help.

Acceptance is the goal toward which all the foregoing grief reactions are moving. But when it begins to appear, it often vanishes again quickly. One week your parents may seem to be feeling pretty good about you and life, and the next week, unaccountably, they are back to all the old struggles. You may breathe a sigh of relief the first time your parents *finally* seem to have accepted you only to find the next time you see them or talk with them on the phone or get a letter from them they have fallen back into denial, guilt, depression, and so on. "Won't they *ever* accept me?" you wonder.

You may be able to deal with these shifts more calmly if you realize that grief reactions do not progress in a neat and orderly fashion. Your parents are likely to ricochet around among the various aspects of grief, living through each of them not only once, but many times and in no predictable order. Yet if they have touched on acceptance once, they will probably touch on it again and perhaps hold on to it longer the next time. One hopes the time will come when their grief work is completed and acceptance becomes their permanent possession.

Your awareness of the process in which your parents are involved can help you to be patient as they work through their feelings. If parents realize they are in the throes of grief and have some idea of what to expect, they are not as likely to panic but will understand that their feelings of guilt, anger, and depression are normal. These are not comfortable feelings, but at least they are normal. In time their intensity will subside, and what was once the sharpest pain will either be gone or remain only as a dull, residual ache.

Time by itself is not a complete healer, but often the passage of time does lessen the original pain. Time should not be reckoned in weeks or even months, but rather in half years and years. Do not expect today what is appropriate six months or a year from now.

Does any person ever learn the lesson of patience completely? Probably not. But if you allow your parents time to work through their flood of feelings and if they give themselves time to do this, several years from now you may both be surprised and pleased with the results.

Chapter 4

Getting Ready to Make the Big Announcement

Now that you, as a lesbian or a gay man, have some idea of what reactions to expect from your parents when you tell them of your same-sex orientation, let us look at your preparations for telling them and some methods you can use to convey your information.

Do Not Hint

One way *not* to come out to your parents is by dropping hints in your conversation. Many same-sex-oriented persons use this indirect method, thinking that in time their parents will put all the hints together and draw the obvious conclusion. In most cases this technique does not work. Your parents may have been putting bits and pieces of casual information together—or they may not. It is amazing how parents can overlook and ignore those things in their children that they do not care to deal with. Unless your parents really seem to be picking up on the clues you drop, do not expect much from this type of advance preparation.

Some same-sex-oriented persons unconsciously carry

on a variation of this form of coming out. Without knowing it, they drop broad hints and clues in their conversation. One young friend of mine was unwisely scattering inferences about her sexual orientation to her colleagues in a career situation that would end abruptly if her co-workers began paying close attention to her repeated hints. Another friend and I pointed out to her the seriousness of what she was doing. In time she came out to her mother (her father is dead) and to her supervisor. Because this greatly eased the pressure she had been feeling, she no longer had an unconscious need to hint about her lesbianism.

Role Reversal

Generally, the advice regarding coming out to parents has been relatively simple: Wait until you yourself feel comfortable about your sexuality, present the information in as kind a way as possible, supply some helpful reading material about homosexuality, and then hope for the best. These are all good ideas, but you can do a lot more to help them and yourself.

As you prepare to come out to your parents, it is important for you to recognize a fact so basic and so obvious that you may have overlooked it. You have had time—perhaps a long time—in which to prepare to make the announcement to your parents about your sexual orientation. You can choose the occasion, the place, and the method of telling. Your parents cannot.

Between one minute and the next their world changes. Suddenly, your parents' role and your role are reversed. All through the years of your growing up your parents cared for you because they had more information about the world than you did. Now the positions are reversed. Now *you* are the one who has more information about same-sex orientation, and you will have to care for your parents as they move into this area that is new to them. Of course, you will not be a "parent" to them in the same way they were to you when you were growing up. You do need to be the guide, however, in the unfamiliar territory to which you are introducing them.

As discussed in chapter 3, your parents will probably experience grief reactions; perhaps these reactions will be intense. Almost certainly they will have no idea that their words and feelings in response to your information *are* grief reactions. You must be prepared to help them understand their feelings, because at first you may be the only person available to do this.

Many parents, when they learn of their children's same-sex orientation, feel isolated, cut off from their usual world. They have no way of knowing that millions of other parents also have same-sex-oriented children and that therefore they are not alone. All they know is that they have been thrust into a world where everything is new and strange. Worst of all, it seems impossible for them to talk to anyone about what has happened.

Among your parents' friends and acquaintances there may be no one who can help them at this point. The usual people you might suggest may not be equipped to handle the situation. For instance, many pastors, priests, and rabbis have not dealt with their own feelings concerning homosexuality and could not therefore help others. The only thing your parents might be told is that you are a sinner and that they should pray for you and encourage you to seek help in order to change. They might not fare much better if they seek help from their doctor. Even if the doctor has the inclination to attend to emotional as well as physical problems, she or he may not have up-to-date information about homosexuality. Or the doctor may be uncomfortable with this subject. As for your parents' talking with a close friend, this may not be practicable. Most of their friends are not any better equipped to deal with the subject than they are. In addition, there are the questions of whether the friend would keep the information confidential and whether the friend might reject your parents. As you can see, even though you are the one who has precipitated the crisis, you have great potential for serving, at least in part, as a healer.

One way you can prepare is to learn about grief. Check the library and the bookstore for books on the subject, and read one or two. Several books dealing with grief that you might find helpful are listed in "For Further Reading."

If a counselor, your pastor, or an older friend is available, talk with him or her about grief. If you cannot explain to the person what you are planning to do and why you want to talk about grief, find someone else with whom you can be honest.

Another direction your preparation might take was indicated in chapter 2: Learn why families behave as they do. Read one or more books on the subject, and possibly consult a counselor if the relationships in your family seem particularly difficult.

Preparing Through Imagination

An important aspect of your preparation involves acting out what you think is going to take place when you tell your parents. What words are you going to say? Try them out in your mind or, better yet, on paper. You may want to write down what you would like to say so you can work with it from several angles.

What do you want to accomplish in this encounter with your parents? All you can hope to do in this initial session is to share yourself straightforwardly, lovingly, and confidently, and then be available to help your parents begin to deal with the information. Therefore, consider the impression your words will create. You can readily understand that if you say, "Dad and Mom, I have something I want to tell you that may upset you," you are setting the stage for one kind of reaction. But you are setting the stage for a different kind of reaction if you say, "Dad and Mom, I've been wanting to share something with you for sometime because it's pretty important to me and because you two are pretty important to me." This approach does not guarantee they will receive your news gladly, but you *have* conveyed two positive messages: You have told your parents that the information means a lot to you and that you care about them.

Do not string out your introduction with an overabundance of words or talk around what you want to say. This will give the impression that what you have to say is so awful you are trying to postpone the telling. A short lead, in which you use a past experience as a point of contact, may be helpful, such as, "You know you've asked me from time to time about girl (boy) friends, and I've always kind of put you off." Move on at once to, "The time didn't seem right then to say what I want to tell you now, that I'm gay (lesbian)." Or: "Remember when we had that big discussion about homosexuality? Were you aware that I was the one who brought it up?" Continue with something like, "The reason I wanted to talk about homosexuality is that I'm very much interested in the subject. You see, I'm lesbian (gay)."

Having decided what you want to say to break the news to your parents, you now want to imagine a range of possible reactions they may have to your news. Perhaps they will react quite differently from the scenarios you create. Imagining a number of possible responses, however, should make you more surefooted in dealing with whatever situation arises.

Imagine one way your parents might respond. How would you feel if they reacted this way? Would you be angry? Tearful? Panicky? Even though none of these reactions would be helpful in the actual situation, just realizing that you might have these feelings can be useful; they are clues to the unconscious interaction between you and your parents. Why do you feel angry or tearful? What are you afraid of?

On the contrary, in response to your parents' reactions, you may wish you had a short, punchy retort that would put them in their place. Such a response could not possibly bring any of the results you are aiming for in this encounter. Why do you want to retaliate with a sarcastic or wounding reply? Sarcasm is a hostile reaction that can inflict pain or cause angry feelings to escalate.

This type of imaginative work can be upsetting and emotionally draining, but in the long run it could make a significant difference in your family's final accommodation to the news. In your imagination try out as many possible reactions from your family as you can think of and your responses to these reactions. You may do this in your head, on paper, or with a wise, patient, and understanding friend. (Be sure not to choose friends who have axes of their own to grind!)

The point of this exercise is to weed out all the unthinking responses that can undermine what you are trying to do. An angry response from you is not apt to cause your parents to change their minds. More likely it will generate a response that is angrier and shriller than yours, which in turn will probably generate a one-up response from you, and you and your parents are off to a needless, first-class family row.

As you try out various imagined scenarios, do you find yourself feeling like a naughty child, cowering before disapproving parents? You may discover that you are still trying to earn their approval, that you still feel the need to be the best little boy or girl in the world. This, as well as all your other possible reactions, is important information for you as you think about coming out to your parents.

Time, Place, Cast of Characters

Now that you have considered the *content* of your initial coming-out encounter with your parents, let us look at some of the actual methods you can use to convey your information, such basic considerations as time, place, and cast of characters.

There is probably no gay man or lesbian who is not familiar with the horror stories about how some parents have reacted when they found out their children were same-sex-oriented. Not quite so well known are the parental horror stories about hurtful ways in which children have come out to their parents.

For instance, I have a friend whose gay son chose to come out to her late one night in a busy restaurant. Allison, her son, and a friend of hers had gone to the theater that evening. Afterward, in a noisy, crowded restaurant, her son said to her, in front of her friend, "Mother, I want to tell you I'm gay."

Her immediate reaction to his words was an overwhelming desire to stand up in the middle of the restaurant and scream. Instead, she made her way to the ladies' room, where she vomited and wept. For several weeks she was in a state of shock. Her son made no effort to contact her during this time. After three weeks she pulled herself together enough to contact him and begin bridging the gaping hole he had made in their relationship, not by his being gay, but by the painful way in which he had thrust this information on her.

If he had chosen a quiet time and place to tell her, with opportunity for her to feel emotion in private, to talk with him about it, she would probably not have been thrown into such an acute state of shock. The terrible need to scream, the involuntary reaction of her stomach, the deep feeling of shock that disoriented her for a number of weeks—the intensity of all these reactions might have been substantially lessened if his method of telling her had been more humane.

He was young at the time. Obviously, he was panicked by the task he had set himself or he would not have chosen such an inept way of doing it. This woman is capable of great understanding and compassion, and today, some years later, the breach between her and her son has been mended. They have a good relationship, and she is proud of him.

This incident underscores an important prerequisite for coming out to parents: The more at ease you are with your sexuality, the more healthy your self-esteem will be and the better able you will be to help your parents as you come out to them.

This incident also underscores the importance of choosing a suitable time—a quiet, private, unhurried time with as little chance of interruption as possible. Which location is best? Your parents' home? Yours? Neutral territory? What neutral territory might be available to you that also provides privacy? If there are younger children in your family who do not know you are lesbian or gay, make sure they will not interrupt this time with your parents.

Must you take full responsibility for making all the decisions connected with this first encounter, or is there some way to include your parents in the decision-making process? You might say something like, "I want to talk with you privately about a personal matter—none of the other kids present. When would be a good time and where can we talk?" If one of your siblings already knows and is going to be present as support for both you and your parents, you should, of course, let your parents know that this family member will be included.

Do not invite your parents for a festive event—a lovely gourmet dinner, for example—and then drop your bombshell. You will not soften the blow by doing this. Instead, almost certainly they will be left with the unpleasant feeling of having been cheated and betrayed. You promised something pleasant but delivered something quite different. It is much better to live up to whatever you have implicitly promised.

Consideration of what else is going on in your parents' lives can also be important. If one of your parents has just lost his or her job, if they have just found out that your sister is pregnant although single or that one of your siblings is on drugs, or if they are on the verge of divorce, your coming out to them will work out better, in all likelihood, if you can wait until the acute stage of their crisis has passed. Similarly, the day after Christmas is better than the day before. Let your family enjoy an untroubled Christmas Day. Your parents can deal with your information in a more pressure-free atmosphere after the festivities are over. And do not plan to break the news to them ten o'clock at night—any night.

These last few cautions about the timing of your announcement to your parents depend more on common sense and courtesy than on deep psychological insight. *Your* readiness to make your announcement in no way guarantees your parents' readiness to receive it. They may never be really ready, but they should not be struggling with six other serious problems; the immediate timing and setting should be chosen with as much consideration as possible.

Another way of coming out to your parents involves

having a counselor or psychotherapist present when you do the telling. As with any method, there are pros and cons. Your parents should know ahead of time that a counselor will be present. Perhaps the simplest and most truthful explanation would include the information that you have talked with a counselor and that it would be helpful if he or she could sit down with you and your parents to discuss a few matters. Mentioning the counselor as a "friend," or inviting your parents without mentioning the counselor has the drawback of leaving your parents unprepared for the presence of this person who is a stranger to them and, again, could leave them feeling duped. This is a consideration you must weigh as you decide how to get them together with the counselor.

The counselor or therapist should be one in whom your parents could reasonably be expected to have confidence. If your parents are conservative, for instance, a male counselor who wears an earring could conceivably fail to inspire them with confidence in the validity of his judgment, because they would immediately peg him as "the enemy," recruited to brainwash them. A sensitive, low-key person, however, who *hears* them nonjudgmentally and gives them an opportunity to express their real feelings may be effective in defusing a potentially explosive situation. Some parents might feel comfortable with the additional, trained person present. Other parents might feel that any psychological-type person is suspect, and his or her presence would make a touchy situation even worse. Again, you have to weigh the possible reactions of both parents and make your choice. And if you guess wrong, do not berate yourself. You need have no regrets, no "if onlys," no feeling that "I should have *known* it wouldn't work." You are not a fortune-teller or a mind reader. You are trying to help your parents in a situation you think might be difficult for them, and if it does not turn out as you hope, you are not to blame and neither are they. You have no guarantee that the results would be any better if you told them without the counselor present.

Dealing with Your Parents' Responses

Up to this point the emphasis has been on the feelings and reactions you become aware of within yourself as you imagine the encounter with your parents. Now let us look at various reactions you imagine they may have. For instance, what will you do if they respond with anger? Or tears, guilt, blame, shock? Suppose they respond *too* well: "We've suspected it, dear, and we're glad you told us." And then they change the subject. Possibly—just possibly—real acceptance? If this is the case, they probably figured out your sexual orientation long ago and have been waiting for you to tell them.

Try to listen to the underlying message their words convey. For instance, anger that lashes out at you may really be anger at themselves, at their supposed failure as parents, displaced onto you. Denial may be their way of saying, "Give us time." Whatever your parents' reactions, they should not be taken as a definitive statement of how your parents are going to feel about you for the rest of their lives. Different people react to shock and pain in different ways.

All that is necessary in this encounter, after you have given your information, is for you to listen sympathetically and let your parents ventilate their feelings. Are they angry? All you need to say is, "You seem to be feeling a lot of anger, and that's understandable to me." Tears? A more appropriate response than "Don't cry" might be, "I think I can understand your sadness." Expressions of guilt? "I can understand why you feel guilty, but there's no need to blame yourselves because being gay (lesbian) isn't any-body's 'fault.' It's something that just happens." And so on.

"Wait a minute," you may be thinking. "Shouldn't I try to stop their feelings of anger or their tears?"

No. At this stage your parents need acceptance of their feelings, not attempts to deny them. They need to hear you say that the feelings they are experiencing are normal. Ira Tanner says, "If another values our feelings, we 'own' them within ourselves and do not deny the grieving process."[1]

As I mentioned earlier, because you may be the only person available, you may have to serve, at least for a time, as the validator of their feelings. It is important for you to realize that by doing so you are not assuming blame for their *anger, tears,* or *guilt.* You are saying only that these are real and normal *feelings* for this period of their grief process.

But suppose your parents say practically nothing or change the subject. Try to draw them out: "How do you feel now that you know I'm lesbian (gay)?" If they do not respond, do not force them. Talking may come later.

If they respond with misinformation and stereotypes about homosexuality, brief and unemotional statements will do far more good than heated denials: "Statistics show that there are many more heterosexual than homosexual child-molesters." "A lesbian (gay) life-style isn't always promiscuous." "A gay (lesbian) person doesn't have to have a lonely old age." Even though your parents may seem to brush your statements aside, later they are more likely to remember and think about what you have said than if you get into head-to-head combat over their ideas or give them a lengthy and involved lecture.

What your parents may be trying to express, in addition to their grief and shock, is that they care about you and want the best for you. Your parents are not your adversaries. Rather, they are persons you love who are in pain, and you want to help them deal with their pain.

Wrapping It Up

How are you going to conclude this meeting with your parents?

Try to sum up the tone of the encounter *briefly*. "This seems to have been pretty upsetting to you, and I think that's understandable. I was pretty upset six years ago when I realized I was gay (lesbian). Maybe we can talk more about this later, when you've had time to think about it." Or: "You seem to have taken my news pretty calmly, but you may have some other feelings later. Lots of parents do. It's sort of a delayed reaction. If you do feel bad later, let's talk about it."

Let them know it is OK for them to have negative feelings and that it is not going to throw you if they do. Also, leave the door open for further dialogue. You may want to point out to them that parents almost universally suffer grief reactions on learning of their chidren's homosexuality. If they are in an acute stage of reaction, maybe all you will want to do is convey to them that it is all right for them to have these feelings, that many parents *are* upset, confused, in pain, when they are told such news.

Be sure to relate—again—that you have told them you are gay (lesbian) because you love them and do not want barriers between you and them. A hug, a kiss, an arm around their shoulders, a warm touch may be reassuring to them. But perhaps they may not want you to touch them, as if you were suddenly a carrier of the plague. This may hurt you deeply, but if you have mentally prepared yourself for this possibility, you need not be thrown by it. If they shy away from physical contact, respect their wishes without comment. Confine yourself to an expression of verbal caring. You can give way to tears if you want after you have left them.

Time may take care of this problem of being treated like a leper. If it does not, let them know later that their hands-off policy hurts you. This could open up discussion of the notion of same-sex-oriented persons as untouchables and could provide an opportunity for an exchange of feelings.

If you want to let them know immediately that their not wanting any physical contact with you hurts you, remember this standard advice: Do not say, "*You* did thus and so." Talk of *your* feelings: "I feel rejected when you . . ." They may be so involved in their own pain that they give no thought to your pain at their physical rejection of you.

Possibly, you may have no problems in this area because your family members have never expressed their feelings of love by physical contact or by words. You will have to decide whether or not you want to go against your family's unspoken rules and indicate your feelings. By thinking and planning ahead you will be able to go into the encounter with more confidence than if you do not prepare.

Practice various possible dialogues over a period of a few days, a week, a month—whatever timetable you feel you need. The words you actually say when the encounter does take place will probably be very different from those you planned, because you are becoming comfortable in your new role of helper, validator, and comforter in this situation.

Additional Considerations

Words, tones of voice, facial expressions, and actions are powerful tools in conveying one's real meaning to others. The right words may be ruined by voice, expression, or action. You might find it interesting to say, "I love you very much" while standing in front of a mirror. Try saying these words with a loving feeling; then say them in anger, with boredom, jokingly, and in a businesslike way. Match your facial expressions and actions to your tone of voice. Now try mixing, for example, the facial expression of anger with actions suggesting boredom, but still using words about love, and you will see that you are sending contradictory messages. Which are to be believed—your words, your tone of voice, or your actions?

You can have everything else right but wound deeply or arouse anger—or calm inflamed feelings—by your choice of words and the way you state what you want to say. A soft answer still turns away wrath. Listen to yourself, how you phrase ideas, which words you choose. Listen to the words others use, and analyze why some persons automatically arouse your ire, while others make you glad to have encountered them.

Words *can* wound. Words can also heal. They will be important in your continued dealings with your parents.

But suppose you do lose your cool in this or any other encounter with your parents. All need not be lost. An apology is not a sign of weakness. It can be a sign of inner strength and can sometimes open doors that otherwise might have remained closed. Your expression of regret should be for losing your temper or for making a sarcastic or cutting remark. Apologizing is not synonymous with groveling, and you should ask to be pardoned for your actions only, *not* for a deeply held opinion—and certainly not for being gay or lesbian in the first place.

What do you do if your parents start asking you difficult questions, such as, "How do you have sex?" or "Tell me about your first sexual encounter," or "How many women (men) have you had sex with?" There is no good reason to describe your first sexual encounter to your parents or to tell them the number of different persons with whom you have had sexual experiences. A brief statement of your feelings is all that is necessary, such as, "Sex is kind of a private matter. I wouldn't feel comfortable discussing the details of your sex life or mine."

Later perhaps one of your parents may sincerely want to know how same-sex persons "do it." One gay man I know has discussed the mechanics of homosexual sex with his father because his father genuinely wanted to know. Conversely, the mother of a lesbian asked her daughter, in anger, to describe a sexual encounter. The daughter, to punish the mother, did as she was asked. Obviously, much anger existed between this mother and daughter, and both question and answer were expressions of a larger problem between the two.

If your parents ask you if you have a lover and you do, you can say, "Yes, it's Jim (Julia), and someday I'd like you to meet him (her)." In this initial encounter a long, drawn-out discussion of lovers can only be a distraction from the main purpose of your meeting, and if your parents do not bring up the issue, there is no need for you to introduce it now. Later will be time enough.

Phone, Letter, or Proxy?

So far only a face-to-face encounter with your parents has been discussed. What if you want to come out to them, but you cannot be with them? Should you write a letter? Would it be better to tell them on the phone? Or should you have someone else—for instance, a brother or sister—break the news to your parents?

Any of these methods might make good sense, depending on your particular situation. Any of these methods could also be used as a way of avoiding face-to-face encounter, a means of distancing yourself from your parents and from the full impact of their possible anger and pain. You may not yet be secure enough in your sexual orientation to deal with their reactions in person, in which case perhaps you should postpone the telling, if your situation permits.

If you tell your parents on the phone, you have to depend on their words (and perhaps their silences or tears) to provide you with information about their feelings. Visual information is lacking. If you tell them in a letter, you cannot offer them immediate help and support. If someone else tells them, you lose the personal interaction between you and your parents at an important time in both your lives. This method may also give them the nonverbal message that a same-sex orientation is so unacceptable you cannot bear to confront them with this flaw in yourself.

If you feel, after considering the various options, that delegating the telling to someone else is the best way in your particular situation, make sure your parents understand why you feel this way. You might consider writing a letter the intermediary could read to your parents, as one young man did with positive results.

As for coming out in a letter, there may be good reasons this makes sense in your particular circumstances. For instance, you may be on the opposite side of the continent from your parents, and it may be imperative that you get this information to them. You may prefer writing to them instead of phoning because yours is a family in which expressing oneself in writing is easier and more natural than emotional verbal encounters. My personal course of action, if I were in this situation, would be to secure a copy of *Understanding Gay Relatives and Friends*,[2] by Clinton R. Jones, steep myself in the tone of the coming-out letters contained in that book, and model my communication along those lines. By writing a letter you have the advantage of selecting just the right words, without the risk of losing them in the nervous excitement of the meeting.

In discussing coming out in a letter with two parents

whose daughter used this method, I found it interesting that the father's and mother's reactions were different. The young woman was away at college but came home frequently on weekends, so it would have been easy for her to tell her parents in person. She chose, however, to write a letter. To the mother, it was a natural thing for her daughter to do this, because the young woman was interested in writing and often used this means of expressing herself. To the father, however, using a letter indicated that his daughter was not comfortable with her sexuality. Because of his questions about her self-acceptance, the parents immediately drove to her college, a four-hour trip, in order to talk with her and assure her of their love and acceptance of her.

Earlier I referred to a young man—Rick—who used the combination of a letter and an intermediary. Rick had come to the point of wanting to come out to his family. He knew the family members would be together for Christmas Day in the midwestern city where they lived, but he could not be with them. Previously, he had come out to one of his brothers, who proved to be supportive. Accordingly, Rick arranged with this brother that, on Christmas evening, he would read a letter from Rick to the assembled family (see Appendix 1). Rick would be waiting by his phone in New York in case any family members wanted to call and talk with him after the letter had been read.

In this family's case the plan worked well. The family *did* call Rick, and each member—mother, brothers, and sisters-in-law—talked with him. Looking back, after several years, his mother felt that Rick's way of telling them "was well thought out, and the proper groundwork was laid. . . . [The letter] answered so many questions and explained so many things that had occurred—especially in the preceding year. He [had] seemed distant and often noncommittal about his activities." She summed up her feelings by saying, "For us, Rick used a good method of communication."

Worst-case Scenario

Inevitably, one comes to the worst possibility, that which every gay and lesbian person has probably had nightmares about at some time: "Suppose my parents throw me out, disown me." This reaction occurs in fewer cases than the prevalence of this fear suggests. Yet it does occur frequently enough that the possibility cannot be discounted.

Usually, when one thinks of parents disowning a child, the reference is to a material and legal disinheriting. It is also possible for parents to disown a child emotionally, even though they may not cut off the child's formal inheritance. Just as emotional divorce can exist between persons who remain legally married to each other, so can emotional divorce exist between parents and a gay or lesbian child.

If, as time goes by, you become aware of an estrangement between you and your parents that grows more and more unbridgeable, you will need to grieve over the withdrawal of your parents' love. If it seems to you that I mention grief incessantly, you are right. You are dealing with change and with many different types of loss, and each change or loss needs to be felt, dealt with, and given due attention if you are to maintain good mental health.

Suppose your parents disown you. What would you do? If this reaction is at all likely, you need to deal with it in two ways. One is a practical approach. How would this action change your life? Would it affect your place of residence, your ability to support yourself? If so, what contingent plans could you make? If you are young and still living at home and this reaction is a possibility, you may want to rethink your decision to come out to your parents.

If you still feel you must come out at this time, you had better do some serious, realistic thinking and planning. Crashing with the first person who offers you space may turn out to be disillusioning, and hustling is a hard and dangerous way to make a living.

The other type of preparation you need to make is emotional. Although no one can be totally prepared for possible emotional trauma, recognize ahead of time that rejection by your family cannot help but be extremely painful. Be aware that you will experience grief reactions over a prolonged period—at least a year, if not longer. If you try to avoid grief, if you do not allow yourself to experience it, if you pretend it is not there, if you do not spend time grieving, you simply postpone the day of reckoning. Initially, you may think you can bypass the normal cycle of grief. You may deceive your conscious mind, but you never deceive your body or your inner, unconscious self. Grief undealt with can cause many different kinds of future problems—physical or psychic or both. It is better for you to do your grief work—and it *is* emotional *work*—at the appropriate time. In so doing you can pick up the threads of your life and encounter less ultimate disruption than if you attempt to ignore your grief.

In chapter 3, I mentioned briefly Beth Jarrett's reaction to the loss of her older son in *Ordinary People*.[3] Her younger son, Con, also reacted strongly and much more immediately. As the story unfolds it becomes apparent that Con did not allow himself to acknowledge and experience the grief of losing his brother and the guilt and shame he felt for surviving while his older brother did not. Because the guilt and shame were false—in the sense of not being realistically deserved—does not mean the feelings were less violent or devastating. They were so intense in fact that he attempted suicide. An experienced gay male counselor told me that many of his clients identified with the younger son's reactions because his inner life closely paralleled their own.

If your parents do disown you, whether legally and emotionally or only emotionally, you are likely to feel a great deal of guilt and shame in addition to your sadness at your loss. Again, the guilt and shame are false, undeserved. A same-sex orientation is not in itself a cause for such feelings, even though society tries to tell you it is.

How can you deal realistically with the devastating grief of parental rejection? On the one hand, you do not want to react with such complete abandonment to grief that you cannot function. On the other hand, to stifle your feelings and deny them so completely that you experience no grief at all is not healthy. Somehow you have to find a way that includes allowing yourself to face your real feelings of pain, anger, depression, and so on, while still managing to cope with the problem life has handed you.

When I was in therapy my counselor gave me some tips on how to feel and cope. "You don't have to allow yourself to be inundated with grief all the time," she told me. She suggested I set aside some time—once a day, twice a day, several times a week, whatever seemed necessary—and give myself up to my feelings for this period. It might be five minutes or a half hour. During the rest of the time, if grief feelings assailed me, I could assure them that if they waited until evening or whenever the next grief period came, I would let them express themselves fully. It may seem odd to you to address your feelings as separate from you, but it *does* work. During the period of your grief, if you find the feelings taking over in an unhealthy way—for instance, with self-destructive thoughts or a need to inflict physical pain on yourself—you can tell your feelings, "That's enough now. I'll come back and grieve tomorrow." You *do* need to acknowledge your feelings and give them a place in your life. You do not, however, need to allow them to take over your life. If self-harming thoughts continue to come, make every effort to seek responsible counseling. If you are still incapacitated by grief after a considerable period, you may also want to consider therapy. This is not weakness. Such a decision can demonstrate strength and wisdom.

Rejection by those whom we rightly expect to love us is an extremely painful experience. As far as you are able, remember that the rejection says more about your parents' problems than it does about you. They have rejected you, not because you are inherently unlovable, but because of their own insecurities, their own fragile hold on their self-esteem. If they did not disown you before they knew you are lesbian or gay, it is not *you* they are disowning, but what they see as a threat to themselves. This rationale may not appreciably diminish the pain for you, but it may help you keep a needed perspective.

If you have the courage and the inner resources, keep the door open to your parents. After some time has passed—three months, six months, a year—if you can and want to do it, make contact with them and ask how they are feeling. A cataclysmic decision, reached in the first shock of finding out about your sexual orientation, may not be the decision they want to live with the rest of their lives. Can you forgive enough to try a tentative overture to them? Do you want to? Feel your way carefully. Do they want you back so they can vent their feelings on you? Do you want to return to the fold because you have a need to receive their condemnation? Or have they grown in the interim? Have you grown? Proceed with caution, and examine your reactions and theirs as objectively as possible. There has to be a balance between your need for self-preservation and your parents' needs, whatever they may be. Move warily but not bitterly or cynically.

Limited Relationship

You may have to settle for a limited relationship. I was much older than I should have been before I realized that my mother was too involved in my life, and that I could not confide all my actions to her unless I was prepared to accept endless streams of advice about the way I conducted my life. She did not hesitate to let me know if she thought I was too involved in church work or that my garden was too big for me to take care of or that I ought to feed my family more or less of certain foods. Obviously, what she worried about had nothing to do with the deeper issues of life. She simply wanted to continue to control me.

Her reasons, if she could have formulated them, would have been complex indeed. To retain a sense of self-worth, she needed to control every situation. She had to have the final word. Because of circumstances beyond her control very early in life, she had been gravely wounded psychologically, and because she grew up in a time when psychiatric help was not a possibility for most people, all her life she remained an emotional cripple.

For me to survive emotionally and maintain my own mental health, I had to determine how I could relate to her without damaging my own ability to cope with life. I discovered that if I wanted to survive as a (healthily) independent person, I could not confide all my day-to-day activities to her. I would have to communicate only those things that were noncontroversial.

I think the reason I continued to confide everything to her long after I should have quit lay in my unconscious programming. As a child, I had absorbed the idea that good little girls told their mothers everything. I did not question this idea for a long time, because I was not aware that this was what I thought. You cannot change what you think until you become aware that you are thinking it.

The necessity for a limited relationship with parents may stem from causes that have nothing to do with sexual orientation. Parents bring their own problems to the task of raising their children. Be aware of this so you do not assume guilt for everything that goes wrong in your relationship with your parents. Every relationship is a joint enterprise. One party alone is not responsible for the interaction and the success of a relationship. Both must work at it.

Hidden Anger

One aspect of coming out does necessitate a considerable amount of soul-searching on your part if you are to avoid wounding your parents and perhaps alienating them permanently. Most of this chapter has been concerned with telling your parents of your sexual orientation because you love them and want to share your complete, real self with them. You should also realize that sometimes motives for coming out are not entirely loving and kind. They may in fact spring from deeply buried anger and pain.

Let us go back to the time when the lesbian or gay person is beginning to realize "I *am* different. I *am* lesbian (gay)." A dismaying host of feelings begins to confront the same-sex-oriented person: fear of his or her emerging sexuality, which seems so different from that of his or her peers; the painful realization that he or she is part of a despised and outcast minority; anger at having to deal with this immense, unasked-for problem; guilt at being the awful person society says he or she is. In this maelstrom of pain the young person thrashes about, looking for reasons why this has happened, looking for someone to help carry the crushing load of shame and guilt.

Just as society has provided your heavy burden through its lesbian and gay stereotypes, so it also provides the scapegoat: your parents. This has happened to you because of your father, your mother, the family system, the home in which you grew up. You are suffering because of *them*. If only you could somehow get back at them for what they have done to you.

And, of course, you can by letting them know what kind of person you really are. You can vent your anger by shattering the image they have of you and letting them know how different your values are from theirs.

Naturally, you do not reason this out in logical sequence, as I have done here. The ideas are mostly hidden from yourself in a murky cloud that whirls and seethes below the surface of your mind. What you do and say is not consciously planned. It simply seems to happen. All of us tend to siphon off unconscious anger in many ways—a sarcastic remark, picking a fight, quiet stubbornness, choosing to do the opposite of what someone wants us to do. In *The Angry Book* Theodore Isaac Rubin has detailed the many ways in which hidden anger leaks out.[4]

There are other sources of pain for the same-sex-oriented person who is becoming aware of his or her sexuality. Because the parents automatically deal with their same-sex-oriented child as a heterosexual person, the child has a vague, undefined sense of not having his or her needs met, as if he or she were forever holding out a hand to the parents and the parents were forever reaching for the child's hand in a different place. Parents and child never seem to connect. Eventually, a feeling—probably not even articulated—builds up in the same-sex-oriented person that "they have never been the parents to me that I really needed. They haven't given me what I longed for."

Gradually, the parents become the adversary. If they sense something different about their child, if they unconsciously sense pain or questioning or asking, they may—equally unconsciously—try to reduce their and their child's anxiety by suggesting remedies that are not remedies. To sons: "Why don't you go out for the baseball team?" "Gym class can't be that bad." "Why don't you ask Sally for a date to the prom?" Or, to daughters: "Wouldn't you rather have some dancing lessons instead of so many team sports?" "But you look so nice in that ruffled blouse." "Maybe you shouldn't have broken up with Bob."

Even though the parents are just trying to help, every time they attempt to move the child in the direction of male or female heterosexual stereotypes, the same-sex-oriented child may perceive the parents as insensitive and authoritarian. It is hardly their fault that they are doing it all wrong.

In a sense no parents give—or even *can* give—their children everything they want in an emotional way, no matter what the sexual orientation of the children. But often gay and lesbian children have a special feeling of being cheated by their parents because the homosexual part of them was not loved and accepted. How could this be? The parents had no way of knowing this part of their child. Even the child may not have understood at that point how she or he was different, only that something seemed vaguely to be missing or out of kilter in life. Because of these feelings of frustration, of anger, of loss that build up in the same-sex-oriented person as she or he grows up, the adult child may come out to the parents in a way that creates distance and vents unconscious anger.

How are you going to know whether you are angry at your parents? It may not be easy, because often such anger is largely unconscious and therefore hidden. For a time, monitor your thoughts about your parents, the ways in which you speak of them to other people, the general tenor of your dealings with them. Is there a persistent undercurrent of irritation, rebellion, hostility, sarcasm, opposition, devaluation? Does it seem impossible for them to do *anything* right?

If you detect some hidden feelings of anger, do whatever is necessary to work through these feelings *before* coming out to your parents. Only as you bring such feelings to light, acknowledge your anger, feel again the pain of their abandonment of a certain part of you—only as you grieve for what you missed can you get beyond the anger and begin to build a better relationship with your parents. Your anger is real and, under the circumstances of your growing up, it was valid. Now it is time to move beyond your anger, to realize that your parents *could not have known* what was troubling you. They were not intentionally "bad" parents. Most likely they may have been faintly bewildered ones.

Many parental horror stories about the hurtful ways in which a son or daughter has come out to his or her parents have originated in the anger of the child who wanted to get back at the parents. The parents do not know this, and the child may not know it. The trauma of such a coming out can be prevented if you take the time to search your soul diligently to uncover your real feelings. Again, you may need or want to seek professional help as you do this.

Not Too Late

What if you have already come out to your parents in a hurtful fashion? It is not too late to deal with your anger, and then go to them and let them know why you were angry. Tell them you understand now that they could not have known your needs. Also ask forgiveness for your harsh words. Such an action could heal the rift between you. Even if it does not, you have done what you could.

In any coming out there needs to be a time when you talk with your parents about your past feelings, thoughts, fears, and struggles as you first became aware of who you really are and then began to deal with the information. The initial encounter may not be the time for this, but it should be soon afterward. All too often we want our loved ones to react in a certain way, and we expect them to read our minds, to know what we want from them. If they really loved us, we think, they would intuit our desires and respond accordingly. Of course, it doesn't work this way. (If it did, they might be able to read our minds when we did not want our minds read!) You need to express your feelings, to share with them something of your struggle over the years if there is going to be a basis for their understanding of what you have experienced. How can you expect them to understand your feelings if they have no idea what you went through?

To those parents who have been deeply wounded by their lesbian or gay child, I say this: Perhaps the last few pages have given you some insights into why your child behaved toward you in angry, hostile ways. If he or she has not come to you to talk about the pain of his or her growing-up years, perhaps you can introduce the subject. It was not your fault, any more than it was your child's fault. The real culprit is society's continuing cruelty to same-sex-oriented persons, and its misunderstanding, ostracism, and condemnation of a group of people with only one difference from the rest of society. If you and your child can begin to understand that each of you has been at the mercy of society's wrongheaded ideas, you can begin to build a bridge between you instead of a wall.

Every coming out is a risk, a gamble. You have no fool-proof means of predicting your parents' reactions. Embarking on this venture with loving, adequate preparation can help. Although success cannot be guaranteed, the chance of failure can be minimized. Your parents' reactions in the initial encounter are immaterial. What happens in the succeeding months is what counts.

Chapter 5

Working Through Grief—Together

The initial step has been taken. The first encounter with your parents has been accomplished. Whatever the results, neither they nor you will have to go through that particular event again. At times I have been thankful that there is no way of inadvertently getting caught in a time warp and having to live a particular day over.

Where do you go from here? What are the next steps?

Usually, the next step has been for the gay man or lesbian to supply his or her parents with information, lending or giving them whatever books might help them to understand a same-sex orientation. In so doing the gay man or lesbian may be omitting a few important intermediary steps. The parents may not yet be ready to read about homosexuality.

A Peculiar Situation

Remember that your parents are in a peculiar situation. They have entered a grief process for a person—you—who is definitely very much alive, whom they can see, and with whom they can communicate, and that is what creates the problem. This point was touched on in chapter 3, but let us look at it now in more detail. The *you* they thought they knew is gone, and yet the *you* they see and deal with now seems hardly any different. This is why it may be hard for them not to hope that somehow this trauma will vanish and everything will return to the way it used to be. They need to grieve, but it is difficult for them to do this when you are obviously alive and well.

For you, there are unpleasant undertones to their mourning. Even talking about sadness in connection with your sexual orientation indicates that the person you really are is so unacceptable that they need to grieve. Unfortunately, this is the message your parents have gathered from society's attitudes toward a same-sex orientation. It is not their fault they are reacting this way, and your getting impatient with them will not do much to hurry them along or improve your mutual relationship.

Is there anything you can do other than wait for them to work through their grief? Considering that it usually takes two years or longer for parents to accept fully a child's same-sex orientation, you certainly hope so!

Actually, you can do a number of things for your parents.

Several days after the initial revelation of your sexual orientation drop in to find out how they are doing or phone them. Even if it means paying for a 3,000-mile long-distance call, spend the money. There are times when it is better not to economize.

Let them know you are making this contact because you are concerned about *their* welfare, not because you are trying to find out how they are feeling about your sexual orientation. Are they having difficulty sleeping? Eating? If they are, this is not at all surprising, and you can reassure them that their reaction is not unexpected.

If you have not told them that they are most likely experiencing grief reactions, you could tell them now. Perhaps they realize this, but if not, you are the logical person to tell them. Unless they have been able to talk with their minister, priest, or rabbi or their doctor, a counselor, a friend, or other family member—which they probably have not—you are their primary source of help and information.

If they want to talk, be available to them. If not, do not force them.

Helpful Books for Parents

During this period you could offer to lend your parents a book that gives some insights into the general process of working through grief. Even if they have dealt with the death of family members or friends, they may not have been aware of the process through which they passed, and it might help them now to be more conscious of what is going on inside them. It may comfort them to know that their feelings of guilt are *normal* in a loss situation; that anger is not unusual; that there is always the temptation to deny what has happened and that, if the shock has been severe enough, denial may be a real survival mechanism for a time; that some depression can be expected and will pass (if the depression is so acute as to be totally incapacitating, your parents may need the help of a trained counselor in dealing with the situation); and that feelings of acceptance may come and go.

If they are not interested in reading a book about grief, accept their decision and let them know you have one available any time they care to read it.

As time goes on you might suggest they read *Sexual Signatures*, by John Money and Patricia Tucker. It has some nontechnical, helpful information about sexual development in general and includes information on homosexuality that could help alleviate whatever guilt they may be experiencing.

After *Sexual Signatures* you may want to suggest they read one or two other books written specifically with parents in mind: *Understanding Gay Relatives and Friends* by Clinton R. Jones, *Parents of the Homosexual* by David and Shirley Switzer, *Now That You Know* by Betty Fairchild and Nancy Hayward, *Consenting Adult* by Laura Z. Hobson, and my book, *My Son Eric*. In "For Further Reading" I have provided a brief description of each of these books. Either now or later your parents may find *this* book helpful as well. An excellent all-around book dealing with both religious and general aspects of a same-sex orientation is Letha Scanzoni and Virginia Mollenkott's *Is the Homosexual My Neighbor?*

You might think the books that helped you come to terms with your sexual orientation would also help your parents. Experience has often proved different. What met your needs will probably not meet your parents' needs, and the books you found particularly helpful may be all wrong for them. At this point in trying to deal with the information about your sexual orientation, they are more likely to trust heterosexual authors, especially other parents.

Important Source of Information

It is good that you should offer to lend or give books to your parents if they indicate an interest or that you should recommend they obtain such books from a library or bookstore. This should not be a substitute, however, for your willingness to sit down with them and discuss your lesbianism or gayness. You are an important source of information for your parents.

One of the most helpful things you can do for your

parents is give them an opportunity to ventilate their feelings and fears. This may be uncomfortable for you and difficult to deal with. When people direct any sort of negative feelings toward us, our instinctive reaction is to defend ourselves by flinging the negative feelings back at them. When they attack, we deny or counterattack, and before we know it we are on a collision course.

If your parents attack, it is because they are experiencing uncomfortable feelings and are trying to deal with them. If you can realize this and try to interpret their feelings to them—"You're feeling pretty bad about this, aren't you?"—you do not run as much risk of getting into a verbal free-for-all as if you undertake to show them how wrong they are or to change their ideas about you conclusively.

The reverse of this is that you also have a right to express your feelings—"I feel as if you disapprove of me, and that hurts." Trying to change someone or tell him or her what he or she is doing wrong invites trouble. If I can say how *I* am feeling instead of attacking the other person, the way is opened for constructive dialogue. An honest ventilation of feelings rather than accusations can lead to a more understanding relationship on both sides.

After a while your parents may want to discuss with you their fears concerning a same-sex orientation. Many of these fears may be the old stereotypical ideas, and you may be impatient at having to deal anew with this misinformation. If you can see each erroneous statement they make as an opening for you to present the facts *calmly and objectively*, without hostility or condescension, you may begin to look on their statements and questions as opportunities and welcome the chance to provide more accurate information. Sometimes it may seem that you are not getting through, but if you keep giving them sound information, without a display of anger or annoyance, in time the information—and your attitude—may significantly change their thinking.

Sometimes your anger or annoyance at one or both parents may have less to do with your sexual orientation than with other facets of your relationship with them. I encountered a gay friend at a time when he was distressed with his parents. Both parties had been battling about his orientation for some time without making any progress toward resolution. When I saw him a month later the stalemate had finally been broken. He and his family were in business together, and he had been feeling a great deal of resentment toward his parents, because they had not clearly defined his duties and authority. He was expected to function in whatever ways he was needed, but he had not been told what those ways were. After he explained to his parents the problems he was experiencing in the business, the three of them were able to work out a satisfactory arrangement, and his sexual orientation no longer served as a focus of the problems that had existed between them.

It is easy for parents who have a lesbian or gay child to think that all problems concerning this daughter or son result from the different sexual orientation. This became especially apparent to me in the Families of Gays and Lesbians group. Many times I spoke with distraught parents out of my experiences with my straight daughters rather than with my gay son. This indicates to me that the problem bothering the parents is connected more with the normal friction between parents and child than with difficulties specifically caused by a different sexual orientation. It may be easier to wrangle endlessly about gayness or lesbianism than focus on the real issues, such as freedom and control, which may be more threatening to the parent-child relationship than sexual orientation.

Just Like Anybody Else

What facts about a same-sex orientation might be reassuring to your parents? One of the things that quieted my fears, although I did not realize it until later, was the ordinariness of the life my son and his lover were leading. They went to work in the morning and came home to their apartment at night to cook meals, wash clothes, shop, clean. They began to redecorate the apartment, doing all the work themselves. They went to church on Sundays and to movies, plays, and concerts. Now and then they entertained friends. In spring and fall they would go in with others and have a garage sale. Their life together was so typical of any young couple that it was impossible for me to regard them as strange or alien beings. The Eric I was seeing was no different from the person he had been before I "found out."

You also might reassure your parents and help them understand you by letting them know you have the same needs, feelings, and desires as a straight person. You need food and shelter, work and play, companionship and love. The same things create pain for you that create pain for everyone: loss of a loved one, loss of friends, loss of a job, quarrels with a lover, loneliness, rejection. You may think it is obvious to your parents that homosexual persons do not have one kind of feelings and heterosexual persons another. Yet quite possibly they do not understand that gay and straight persons share the same *kinds* of human feelings. Only the sex of the loved one may differ.

Do not assume that your parents know these basic facts about you, and do not be angry that you may have to tell them you are just like other people. For several thousand years society has been giving them the opposite impression, that same-sex-oriented people belong to some strange and peculiar breed that has no normal human needs or feelings and that is obsessed with thoughts of sex.

It may be reassuring to your parent to know that they are not the *only* ones with a same-sex-oriented child; there are literally millions of parents like them. If you consider that an estimated 5 to 10 percent of the population is same-sex-oriented and that each gay man or lesbian has two parents, you can easily get a rough idea of how many parents are facing or have faced the same questions as your parents. Of course, many parents do not know they have a lesbian or gay child. Many more are not telling other people. Those who are not afraid or ashamed to let others know they have a same-sex-oriented child are comparatively few, which is why your parents may think their situation is unique.

Although your parents may not think so at first, it does help to talk with other people who are going through similar experiences. If a Parents and Friends of Lesbians and Gays group is available nearby, your parents could be comforted, helped, and informed by attending meetings. If no group is organized where your parents live, possibly another set of parents would be willing to correspond with your parents. Although I know of no organized effort to put parents of same-sex-oriented children in touch with one another by mail, this should not stop you. All you need is a gay or lesbian friend whose parents have made some measure of peace with their child's orientation and who would agree to exchange letters with your parents now and then, if they are interested.

It might be helpful to your parents to know that many fine people are lesbian or gay. If one day every same-sex-oriented person turned green, we would soon discover the truth of the placards carried in gay rights parades: "We are everywhere." One would see green doctors, nurses, teachers, priests, pastors, bus drivers, politicians, re-searchers, secretaries, service station attendants, accoun-tants, athletes, assembly line workers, artists, actors, musicians, broadcasters, airplane pilots, flight attendants, computer operators and technicians, police officers, law-yers, judges, and on and on. By far the greatest proportion of lesbians and gay men are leading quietly constructive lives. They are like the great mass of heterosexual people who also live quietly constructive lives. Neither group makes many headlines.

Throughout history same-sex-oriented persons have contributed greatly to the physical, mental, and spiritual welfare of humanity.[1] These include James Miranda Barry, the first British woman doctor, who successfully served the British government all her life disguised as a man; Howard Brown, M.D., New York City's first health ser-vices administrator, the director of community medicine at Fordham Hospital, and head of the Gouverneur Morris Hospital Ambulatory Care Unit on New York's Lower East Side; Rosa Bonheur, a nineteenth-century artist; Erasmus (1466–1536), the greatest scholar of his age and editor of a Greek New Testament; James I of England, who commis-sioned the translation of the Bible that has come to be known as the *King James Version;* and Frederick the Great, who welcomed the persecuted Huguenots to Prussia and abolished press censorship and torture.

There are a host of others, among them poets Thomas Gray, Walt Whitman, Gerard Manley Hopkins, A.E. Housman, and W.H. Auden; authors Marcel Proust, Willa Cather, Henry James, and Edith Hamilton; educators Mary Emma Wooley, president of Mount Holyoke College for thirty-seven years and one of the first American women diplomats, and Carey Thomas, for many years dean and president of Bryn Mawr College; as well as such world famous and instantly recognized names as Leonardo da Vinci, Michelangelo, and Peter Ilich Tchaikovsky. Our lives are richer because of these same-sex-oriented persons and because of those thousands unnamed for lack of space.

Not Child Molesters, Not Recruiters

Demeaning as it may seem, you may have to reassure your parents emphatically that you are not a child molester, nor are you trying to recruit people to a same-sex orientation. If your parents have not already gotten the message that it is impossible to recruit people to a homosexual orientation, you may have to be blunt about this. The idea that children are in danger of being molested by all same-sex-oriented persons has been around for a long time. Anita Byrant's crusade in 1977 to repeal the Dade County, Florida gay rights ordinance gave new visibility, impetus, and status to this already discredited supposition. Your parents need to know it is untrue that every homosexual person is a child molester or a recruiter.

You might also point out, if the occasion arises, that all the fears about homosexual teachers and others as role models for children tend to be exaggerated. Most homosexual children have grown up with heterosexual parents for role models, and many children know they are different (although they may not have a name to put to the difference) long before they reach adolescence or have had any sexual experiences. Approximately 90 percent of the population is heterosexual; thus nine out of ten of a child's role models are heterosexual.

What About Change?

What do you do if your parents talk about change?

First, remember this: *Stay calm.* Even though you may want to ride into battle immediately on this issue, with colors flying, *do not.* Ultimately, you will gain more by courteously listening to your parents than by trying to outargue them.

This does not mean you should agree to go into counseling. It means you need to understand the message underlying your parents' wanting you to change. They may be saying, in effect, that life would be simpler for you and for them if you were not same-sex-oriented. It may be a manifestation of the denial aspect of their grief—"Our child really doesn't *have* to be same-sex-oriented." They may, if they are religiously oriented, be concerned about the eternal damnation of your soul. (This is dealt with at greater length in chapter 9.)

Finally, there is the tantalizing shred of hope that holds—just out of reach—the possibility that same-sex-oriented people *can* change. William H. Masters and Virginia E. Johnson effected changes in some gay men and lesbian women, didn't they? And what about the ex-gay organizations that claim men and women have changed? Lawrence Hatterer, professor of psychiatry at Cornell University, has written about changing homosexuality in men.[2] Recently, a system of study called aesthetic realism has also been attracting attention with claims of having changed same-sex-oriented persons.[3] "See?" your parents are crying to themselves. "It is possible. *It is possible!*"

Possible, perhaps, but not necessarily probable. Years ago researcher Alfred Kinsey and his colleagues developed the Kinsey continuum, popularly referred to as the Kinsey scale.[4] Through research he and his co-workers discovered that besides those persons who were either completely heterosexual or completely homosexual there were those who could function with varying degrees of satisfaction and adequacy in either role.

Because one person can move from a same-sex orientation to an opposite-sex orientation does not guarantee that another person can; the two persons may occupy different positions on the Kinsey scale. One might be closer to the completely heterosexual position and thus have a considerable heterosexual component in his or her makeup, whereas the other might be close to complete homosexuality or else entirely same-sex-oriented.

Concerning Masters and Johnson's work in helping same-sex-oriented persons function satisfactorily in an opposite-sex-oriented way, one has only to read even sketchily in *Homosexuality in Perspective* to realize that they are not presenting a foolproof means for changing all homosexual persons to heterosexual.[5] Applicants for this therapy were carefully screened; the number of persons treated was statistically small; no claims were made that the persons treated were representative of the same-sex-oriented population as a whole. To generalize from their work that because one person could be treated successfully, all could is impossible.

In dealing with the claims of ex-gay organizations consider that there is no accurate way to confirm their glowing assertions. There is no follow-up five or ten years after change to ascertain whether the person is living exclusively as an opposite-sex-oriented person. Many times ex-gay means no more than that a same-sex-oriented person is living a celibate life.[6] Generally, ex-gay claims are strong on assertions of change and appallingly weak on reliable statistics.

As for Dr. Hatterer's statement that he has changed many persons, hopeful parents need to be aware of the earlier caution that because one person can change does not guarantee another can. They also need to know that such changes have necessitated large outlays of time, money, and effort as well as living in the proper geographic location—near a therapist effective in this area of work.

Parents need to be aware of still other considerations in

the matter of change. What does it do to a person's self-concept to say, "I am unacceptable as I am; therefore, I must change" and then realize years later that he or she is going to have to remain "unacceptable" for life because change does not seem possible? Why should a young man or woman spend precious time and precious energy pursuing a goal that may be doomed at the outset? At the end of the years of effort he or she still has to do an about-face. Instead of fighting the same-sex orientation, the person now has to learn to live comfortably, productively, and happily with an unchanged sexuality. Is it fair for parents to force this difficult path upon a person?

There are many books, particularly religious books and articles, that can feed parents' dreams of changing a lesbian or gay child to heterosexual. If parents *must* read such books and articles, they would be wise also to read books with more scientific information, which present a less biased view of the possibilities of change.

Sexual Preference, one of the newer books in this area of concern, demonstrates the great complexity of possible causes of a same-sex orientation.[7] The reader who tries to follow and understand the path diagrams presented in the book will get a glimpse of the tremendously complex interaction of a host of variable circumstances. The book also questions a number of ideas that have been seen as causes of a same-sex orientation and shows that what has been assumed to be *causes* may in reality have *resulted* from a same-sex orientation. For example, the supposition has been that an unsatisfactory father-son relationship could cause a homosexual orientation. Researchers raise the question that if there is a biological basis for a person's same-sex orientation, possibly the estrangement between father and son may result from a perception (probably unconscious) of the child's difference.

Your parents need the foregoing information if they are

serious about wanting you to change. Presenting the information to them without anger, as factual material, can give them the opportunity to hear it without needing to defend their ideas against heated attack. If you can keep your feelings separate from the information you want to give and can handle their and your emotions apart from the giving of objective data, both you and they will have a better chance of dealing constructively with the whole situation. Their dissatisfaction with your sexual orientation is painful to you and may need to be addressed, but it should be dealt with apart from the information that most likely you cannot change.

Two sentences on the last page of *Sexual Preference* should be repeated often, loudly and clearly: "It is possible for both homosexuals and heterosexuals to enjoy mature, constructive, and rewarding lives. Probably each orientation involves its own dangers, sacrifices, and compensations."[8]

Fears About Your Physical Welfare

Perhaps some of the apprehension your parents have may be related to your physical welfare. They may be fearful for your health and safety. If they read newspapers and magazines and listen to radio and TV news they know the incidence of sexually transmitted diseases is higher within the gay male community than within the straight community. They are also aware of the high incidence of violence, whether exerted by those who hate same-sex-oriented persons or by the small percentage within the gay community who are psychopathic.

Your parents' fears about violence are not idle, and their concern for your health and safety indicates they care about you. If you can accept their concern and reassure them that you are dealing with these problems responsibly, this can help their peace of mind greatly.

If you cannot do this, it might be indicative of several things. Your general relationship with your parents may be on such precarious footing that anything seeming to you to be parental meddling arouses angry, combative feelings of which you may not have been conscious, until now. If you become defensive, however, because you *are* doing the things they are concerned about, maybe it is time for you to take stock of yourself.

Let us face it: Sexual pickups can be dangerous because of the risk of contracting sexually transmitted diseases and because of possible physical violence. Other practices, particularly in the gay male community, are also destructive to physical and psychological health, such as the misuse of chemicals and drugs—including amyl nitrite and butyl nitrite—the indiscriminate use of antibiotics, and sadomasochism. If you are involved in this kind of potentially destructive activity, perhaps you should take a second look at yourself and ask why.

Why is there so much cruising and anonymous sex in the gay male community? Many gay men may be unaware of the underlying sociological and psychological reasons. Throughout history society has encouraged heterosexual men to form monogamous relationships with women in order to provide a secure setting in which to produce and raise children and thus perpetuate the human race. Society has been uninterested in encouraging stable, long-term relationships between same-sex-oriented persons for at least two reasons. One is that such relationships were, quite wrongly, considered a threat to the continuation of the race. Unconsciously, people must have believed that if same-sex relationships were allowed, these liaisons would prove so much more fascinating than heterosexual ones that most people would choose a same-sex partnership and population would therefore decline drastically. Stated baldly, the idea sounds ridiculous, as unconsciously held ideas often do. The other reason is that most people did not realize persons of the same sex could have loving, tender, bonding feelings for one another. The assumption was that sexual activity between persons of the same sex resulted only from lust so excessive it could not be satisfied heterosexually.[9] For these reasons neither society nor the church supported or even condoned same-sex relationships.

The same-sex-oriented population, duly indoctrinated with the wrong information it gleaned from heterosexual society, formulated its own behavioral standards. Because sexual contact between two men cannot result in pregnancy, the gay male community saw no reason to limit sexual activity. If it felt good, why not do it? There was no woman to hold back, tone down, or rein in the male sex drive. Interestingly, sexual activity within the lesbian community is quite different from sexual activity in the gay male community. Whether this reveals the difference between male and female socialization or represents different inborn instincts and drives is too complex a question to discuss here. The fact is there *is* a considerable difference.

But repeated, anonymous, or casual sexual stimulation can become a trap. It promises the warmth and real relationship that human beings yearn for, whether they are aware of this yearning or not. Yet this kind of sexual activity cannot fulfill its promise. For the brief time of sexual contact physical and psychological reactions take place that feel good. The brain releases endorphins, the body's own painkiller, producing a natural high. Emotionally, one's ego-boundaries fall and there is a fulfilling sense of oneness and sharing with the partner—for a moment.

Both these reactions may be deceptive. A person can get hooked on the euphoria produced by the endorphins and seek repeated sexual release in order to reproduce this feeling of well-being, never mind with whom. The oneness may be nothing more than an illusion that departs quickly. But if a person has no relationship in her or his life that is producing a *real* closeness and sharing, the temptation is to grab whatever feelings of closeness she or he can, however possible. When this type of fleeting liaison fails, in the long run, to produce a relationship of depth and extended duration, the tendency is to keep searching, thinking that one simply has not found the right person. And so the seeker keeps repeating a behavior pattern that cannot produce the results for which she or he is looking.

There are other reasons for seeking anonymous sex. "I finally realized that the times I went after anonymous sex were when I was really angry," a gay man told a group in a moment of self-disclosing honesty. "It was like I wanted to go out and shoot someone," he said, thumbs cocked and index fingers of both hands extended, as if he were firing two pistols. "Now when I feel like going out and having sex like that, I ask myself what it is I'm angry at, and I try to deal with the anger instead of going after sex."

Some deal with various other feelings by means of promiscuous sexual behavior. Because the true issues in the person's life are being bypassed, they cannot be resolved. Instead, the person repeats the behavior endlessly, always searching for a result the behavior will never produce.

The lesbian or gay man faces other pitfalls that result from her or his being part of an oppressed and mostly outcast minority.[10] To survive, such minorities develop their own rules. The collective gay community lore indicates that a gay man behaves in such and such a way. The lesbian community has also developed its own collective ideas about how a lesbian should behave. In this way minorities draw together and define their difference from the surrounding society that is hostile to them.

This drawing together and defining of differences is at

once strengthening *and* detrimental to the individual lesbian or gay man. On the one hand, it clues her or him in on how a same-sex-oriented person of that gender behaves. On the other hand, it can severely restrict the gay man's or lesbian's choices of behavior to what are basically stereotypical reactions, even though they may be approved by the collective gay or lesbian community.

If you, as a lesbian or gay man, have been reacting according to collective prescriptions, sexual or otherwise, now is a good time to take stock of yourself. Are the choices you are making about your life-style the ones you want to make or are you unquestioningly following the herd? Are you dealing with your emotions and your body in a way that demonstrates caring and respect? Is your behavior constructive or destructive? Are you reacting with self-destructive behavior because of hostile messages from family or society?

Your reactions to your parents' concerns may open up these and equally soul-searching questions. Or your preparations for coming out to your parents may bring you face to face with such concerns. Do not evade the issues; they affect your life deeply. If you grapple honestly with these issues and stick with them until you have satisfied your needs constructively, you will have made giant strides toward a mature, creative, fulfilling life.

Is a Full, Satisfying Life Possible?

Another fear your parents may express is the belief that, because you will not marry and have children, you are doomed to a lonely old age. If your parents express such a fear, a frank and open discussion can help alleviate their dread. Marriage and children are not safeguards against loneliness in old age. A spouse can get a divorce or die. Children may precede their parents in death or may live hundreds of miles away when the parents are old.

Lack of an opposite-sex partner and children does not automatically sentence one to loneliness in one's advanced years. Your parents may not be aware that a long-term, committed relationship can exist between two same-sex-oriented persons and that many such enduring relationships are being maintained. Your parents also may not realize that many older gay men and lesbians, whether single or coupled, have built up a circle of supportive friends, just as older single and coupled heterosexual persons do. Because people are generally living longer, it is important for every person individually—heterosexual or homosexual, married, in a nonmarried relationship, or single—to make realistic plans so that old age is not a time of loneliness.

Your parents may also fear that you cannot possibly live a full, happy life because you will never have a heterosexual spouse and children. (Naturally, this fear will exist only if you have not already been married and had children.) This fear results, at least in part, from cultural conditioning. From the time your parents were children they have perceived marriage and family as the norm for adult life. Although this norm is being questioned vigorously by young adults nowadays, when your parents were growing up the assumptions were that everyone's goal was marriage and that, unless husband or wife was infertile, children would almost automatically follow. For this reason many parents find it difficult to imagine a full and satisfying life is possible on any other basis.

Your first reaction to this kind of thinking may be anger or, less intensely, annoyance: "*Of course* it is possible to have a good life built on bases other than heterosexual marriage and children. Marriage and family were *never* goals in *my* life, and what my parents think will bring me the greatest happiness *doesn't appeal to me at all.*" Is this what you are thinking? If it is, perhaps you should take a second look at this matter. Perhaps this is an area in which you, as a lesbian or a gay man, need to grieve with your parents.

This is not, as you may think, a typical heterosexist idea. It comes from Douglas Elwood, a gay man, a trained therapist who is director of training and education at Lesbian and Gay Community Services in Minneapolis, and a faculty member of the University of Minnesota School of Social Work.

Because all children are assumed to be heterosexual, Elwood says, they are raised with the implied or expressed expectation that in time they will marry and become parents. When lesbians and gay men discover their same-sex orientation, face it, and work through to acceptance of it, they lose the role envisioned for them by society in general, by their parents in particular, and perhaps in their own thinking.

They also lose the approval society bestows on those who conform to its accepted patterns. In the business world the unmarried male is considered unsuitable in many positions, particularly if he is approaching the middle years. While the unmarried woman is not at a disadvantage in the business world, she is nevertheless subject to the strong general suspicion in her personal life that she is not attractive enough to get a man. A great deal of life is organized on the principle of two persons in a couple relationship, and it had better be a male coupled with a female—preferably by marriage. Those who do not conform to the heterosexual couple pattern are penalized in subtle and not so subtle ways, the greatest penalties being reserved for those who differ most from the established standard—same-sex-oriented persons.

Whether you, as an individual, wanted marriage and family or not, you are trading the secure societal role of a heterosexually oriented person for the more insecure position of a member of a stigmatized subculture. You are forfeiting many basic rights and protections that hetero-sexually oriented people take for granted: the right to live, eat, and go to school where you want; the right to enter any career for which you are educationally and tempera-mentally suited; the right to be judged by your knowledge and skill as a worker rather than by your sexual orienta-tion; the right to equal protection under the law.

As you can see, you lose many personal and social rights and advantages as you face and accept your sexual orientation. Why should you not grieve at the heavy penalty exacted from you simply for being who you are?

Possibly the idea of such grieving does not appeal to you. Acceptance of your gayness or lesbianism may have been a difficult battle for you. Perhaps achieving peace with yourself came only after a long and determined struggle. Instinctively, you may fear that if you open the door to grieving for lost heterosexual privileges, you may loose such a flood of sorrow and self-pity that you will be inundated. It may seem better for you to keep the door shut tightly.

In facing and accepting your lesbian or gay orientation you are choosing to live in accordance with your real per-sonhood, rather than attempting to live a hollow charade as a heterosexual person. You are choosing to be true to yourself, because you have realized that only in this way can you find wholeness and satisfaction in life. *Because* you want to live out your particular orientation it is necessary to grieve for the more socially approved avenues of life that are closed to you. In so doing you are not repudiating your given sexual orientation or your decision to live it rather than attempting the lifelong dishonesty and pain of pretending to be heterosexual.

Rather, by facing your loss, allowing yourself to feel it, and coming to a suitable closure you free yourself from wasting emotional energy in various forms of unproductive behavior. Out of such unacknowledged and undealt-with grief comes heterophobia, which may manifest itself in aggressive disparagement of heterosexuality, extreme defensiveness about homosexuality, and anger against anything perceived as a heterosexual value. Out of such unacknowledged feelings of loss may also come such things as alcohol or drug abuse, family problems, relationship problems, self-esteem problems, and ill health. If you have not allowed yourself to grieve, neither will you be able to allow your parents to grieve, and you will not achieve any real family closeness by coming out to your parents. Under such circumstances you may have chosen to come out to your parents in the unconscious hope that they could ease the pain of loss inside you.

A good deal of courage may be required for you to allow yourself to grieve along with your parents, and yet if you can share with them the anger and grief you felt as you faced your own loss, you can help them come to terms with their loss. You are giving them permission to be angry and to hurt because of *their* loss. In other words, you are telling them that their feelings are real and that it is all right for them to have these feelings.

Grief always has a paradoxical aspect. If you allow yourself and others to mourn a loss, you and they will recover from the loss and resume life more fully and healthily than if you repress or ignore your own and their grief. Bypassing grief only ensures your remaining in the process unhealthily and unproductively.

Winning or Losing Together

As you—both children and parents—may have gathered from this chapter, the essence of working through grief as a family lies in facing, acknowledging, and sharing your true feelings and then dealing with them realistically.

This is the ideal. Because we are less than perfect, it is

not always possible to live up to this ideal. Somewhere along the way there will probably be some missteps— raised voices, heated arguments, untenable positions firmly held.

There is a vocabulary that heals such breaches in family solidarity. It includes phrases like, "I'm sorry I lost my temper"; "I shouldn't have shouted"; "I've been thinking about what you said and it seems to make sense"; "Maybe we both need to get more information about this"; "In some cases I guess we have to agree to disagree."

Perhaps the foregoing material has given the impression that while working through grief, every encounter between parents and child must be a heavy emotional scene. This could be wearing. It could also create the suspicion that either or both parties, parents and child, are setting up meetings to hammer away at the other's point of view.

How much better it might be simply to have fun together sometimes, pleasant times when same-sex-orientation is put aside. If you and your parents have been going at it rather intensively, it might be helpful to agree ahead of time that the subject will not be discussed at the next encounter. If it seems uncomfortably formal or blunt to specify this ahead of time, the situation could be dealt with if the subject arises. A leading remark could be passed over (it is not *always* necessary to rise to the bait) or the subject could be put aside with the casual remark that perhaps it could be discussed at another time, that right now you are in the mood to have fun.

You may have noticed that many of the suggestions in this chapter will be easier to follow if you live in the same locality as your parents and meet each other in person from time to time. If you live a distance away, you will have to adapt the suggestions to your particular situation. If you are not in the habit of writing or phoning your parents frequently, it might be well to make more of an effort now to keep in touch. Such thoughtfulness and concern at this time could mean a great deal to them.

You and your parents are bound together in a situation where all of you win together or all of you lose together. You cannot win at your parents' expense, nor can they win at yours. If together you can grieve for your lost role in society and in the family and together lay away the ideas of marriage, children, continuity with future generations, and a secure heterosexual niche in society, both you and your parents will be free to move on to shape an improved parent-child relationship and find the positive aspects of your life as a same-sex-oriented person.

Chapter 6

The Other Side*

If you are a parent reading this book, one week or one month or six months or a year ago you probably experienced a collapse of part of your world when your child told you he is gay or she is lesbian. In a matter of minutes one of the fundamental certainties you had about your child disappeared. Instead of the heterosexual son or daughter you thought you had, you suddenly discovered that in his or her place you have a gay son or a lesbian daughter. The realization may have been a shock to you. Since then you may have been experiencing rather vividly some of the feelings discussed in chapter 3.

If you have weathered the most acute stages of grief, perhaps the time has come to discover what your child has been experiencing since his or her first inklings that he or

*The material in this chapter, unless otherwise indicated, is based directly on "Coming Out Alive, A Positive Developmental Model of Homosexual Competence" by John Grace, coordinator of the Gay and Lesbian Family Counseling Program at Family and Children's Service, Minneapolis, Minnesota. The paper was delivered at the Sixth Biennial Professional Symposium of the National Association of Social Workers and is used here with the author's permission. The lesbian viewpoint has been supplied in consultation with Jennifer Feigal, also of Family and Children's Service.

she was different. As your child has read this book, he or she has spent time trying to understand something of your life experiences and why you may have reacted in certain ways to the information he or she presented to you. It might be worthwhile now for you to reciprocate— to try to understand something of what your child has gone through in coming to terms with his or her sexuality.

The most obvious thing to do is to ask your child when he or she first realized the difference between himself or herself and his or her friends and peers. How did your child feel? How did he or she cope?

In all likelihood your child has gone through a fairly long period of trauma as he or she struggled with the realization of his gayness or her lesbianism. I have yet to meet a gay man or lesbian who decided one day that he or she was tired of being heterosexual and that it might be fun to try being homosexual. Many people think that at some point same-sex-oriented persons *choose* a homosexual way of life rather than one that is heterosexual. The choice is made, these people believe, because the homosexual persons wish to rebel against parents and/or society or because they have been influenced by some "evil forces" or because they were habituated into a homosexual orientation through early pleasurable same-sex experiences with persons of their own ages or with older persons (recruitment, or seduction).

These people have no idea of the years of pain and struggle that are often part of same-sex-oriented persons' realization of their identity as gay men or lesbians. The accounts I have heard all include the dawning awareness of some difference between themselves and their friends, an awareness commonly accompanied by panic or self-loathing and often by frantic attempts to convince themselves that they really are not perverts or monsters.

If there are twenty million homosexual persons in the

country, there are twenty million different stories about how the truth was borne in on each one, often slowly and excruciatingly, that he is gay or she is lesbian. Although many stories are similar, no two are alike. The cold statistics are compiled from individual experiences, each one of supreme importance to the particular person who had to live through those experiences. Each person who is counted as an impersonal number in that twenty or so million is a living, breathing, feeling person struggling to cope with a situation that life, for some unknown reason, has thrust on her or him. These twenty million are ordinary people—your children and mine—who happen to have one characteristic that has made their lives considerably more difficult than you and I, as parents, had envisioned.

I think of a young man I met at a gay party. He had come because the latest in a long line of counselors had suggested that change was probably an impossibility for him and that perhaps, if he got to know some gay men, he might be able to reconcile himself to the fact that he is gay. He had struggled long and valiantly—and expensively—not to be gay, and it had not worked. Now he has found a measure of peace, has formed a circle of friends, and is active in a gay religious group. To a large extent he has accepted the person he is.

I think also of a woman named Debby.[1] As a teenager, she was active in her church. Suddenly, one day, because she admitted she had some feelings for another girl, she was not welcome at the church anymore. A few months later she had a nervous breakdown and spent eight months in a mental hospital.

When Debby was twenty-one she lost a job because her pastor would not give her a character reference after he heard a rumor—actually a false one—that she was sexually attracted to her female supervisor. At this point Debby was ready to kill herself. Later a Lutheran minister worked with her for two years, helping her to come to terms with herself, helping her realize that she could be both lesbian and Christian, even though many churches feel these terms are contradictory. It took Debby a long time to accept her sexual orientation but, fortunately, she succeeded.

I think of another young man I met. Obviously, he was in the throes of a tremendous crisis in his life. "I'm married," he told me, "and I love my wife, but I've discovered I'm gay. I want to stay married, but I don't know if I can." He and his wife had talked with several counselors. They were working on the problem that had engulfed them as maturely and responsibly as possible. Because I talked with this person only one time, I do not know the outcome of his and his wife's struggle. Clearly, if this young man had had his choice, he would not have chosen the situation in which he found himself.

I think of a twenty-nine-year-old woman who was married, with a baby daughter.[2] As she started working with women on women's issues she began to realize that here, rather than in her marriage, her emotional needs were being met. She also began to realize that in her life there had always been primary and intense relationships with women. Eventually, she made the difficult decision to divorce her husband because of her need to live as the person she had finally recognized herself to be.

Despite the fact that each person's story is different, lesbian and gay men usually go through certain definable stages as they become aware of their real sexual orientation and then begin to deal with it.

If you, as a parent, are cognizant of some of the stages through which your child has passed or is passing, you may not be as terrified of what you see him or her living through as you might otherwise be. Also, if you know something of these stages, you may be more able to give understanding and love to your child instead of revulsion and condemnation. You may feel less need to break off the relationship with your child, more able to talk openly with her or him about your feelings, more able to listen to your child talk about her or his feelings.

The coming-out process for a gay man can be divided into five segments: emergence; acknowledgment; crashing out; first relationships; and finally, self-definition and reintegration. These are the stages as John Grace—and many others—have defined them. Some psychologists and social workers use different terms, so that emergence and acknowledgment are reversed and crashing out is termed the search or exploration.

For lesbians, there is often a preemergent stage, characterized by an empty marriage or by promiscuity or by a feeling that they have been created asexual. Because they do not experience the feelings for men that other women are describing, they assume that some sexual component was left out of their makeup and that they are incapable of experiencing the sexual aspect of life as others do. They have no idea that women will trigger the sexual feelings that men have failed to arouse. All this happens because usually women are unaware of their lesbian orientation until they are well into adulthood. Emergence and acknowledgment for lesbians may be followed immediately by a first relationship and only later by a version of crashing out or exploration that is not as exclusively involved with sexual experiences as for their male counterparts.

Emergence

Most gay men go back to age four or five in order to pinpoint when they began to feel excited about other boys or men in their lives, such as a favorite uncle or family friend, a television or movie hero, a character in a novel, a teacher, an older brother's or sister's friend.

Some boys are lucky enough not to be ashamed or uneasy about these early attractions toward men. If no shame exists, possibly the emergence period can be relatively untroubled. One gay man was fortunate enough to be able to say, "As far back as I can remember, I always had feelings of love for other boys and men in my life. This included a lot of affection and physical and sexual intimacy during late childhood and throughout my adolescence. It wasn't until I was nineteen years old and away at college that I first realized all the other men in the world didn't feel the same way I did."

Usually, however, feelings of difference are discovered earlier than age nineteen for men and with more damaging consequences. Suppose, instead of such a comparatively calm acceptance of himself, the boy recognizes early, with shame and fear, that he is different from other boys.

Right here it is necessary to restate clearly where the shame—in both lesbians and gay men—comes from. It is a value judgment attached by society to same-sex orientation, rather than being inherent in the orientation itself.

Because of this fear and shame a vicious cycle develops. The fear and shame foster self-hatred and a feeling of worthlessness, which in turn make the boy—or girl—uneasy with both boys and girls his or her own age and with older people—parents, relatives, teachers, friends. This awkwardness contributes to the self-hatred, and the cycle is off and rolling.

If the boy is unwilling to or cannot take part in the other boys' male activities, he is branded a sissy or, at best, shy. He discovers that he is "bad" no matter what he does. If he plays with boys and does not do it right, this is bad; but if he plays with girls, this is bad too. If his dad cannot make a man of him, he is bad; but if he makes up for this lack by being a good student and thereby gains recognition and acceptance, he is in danger of being labeled a teacher's pet, and this is bad.[3]

If he reacts to the stress of his confusion and fear by becoming sick, whether the sickness is pretend or real, he is bad. If he plays hooky to avoid being verbally or physically picked on, he is bad. If his mother, aware of his pain and frightened and confused by it, offers him support, comfort, and protection and he accepts it, he is bad and *so is she.*

Thus, perhaps even before he can put a name to his difference, he begins learning how to survive in a hostile environment. He learns to survive by pretending to be one person and presenting this public self, this mask to his family and friends and to the world at large. Yet underneath he has a secret, private, real self, the person he intuitively knows himself to be, complete with his sexual and emotional fantasies known, most likely, to himself alone.

The greater the difference between his public and private selves, the more likely he will experience confusion in his identity ("Who am I *really*?") and difficulty and distress in relating to the world. Logical reasons can be given for the large percentage of lesbians and gay men who are chemically dependent. This is true not because lesbians and gay men have weaker characters or are inherently worse than straight people, but because they have had to live with greater internal pressures and pain at younger ages than most other people. If your son or daughter is chemically dependent, understanding and love will help more than condemnation.

For lesbians, the emergent stage is considerably different. In the past, society has been more willing to accept tomboyish girls than effeminate boys. The girl was seen as aspiring to the "superior" status of the male—an understandable action—whereas a boy was seen as downgrading himself by taking on some of the characteristics of the "inferior" female. If a girl's interests lie in tomboyishness, people are not as inclined to suspect a connection between this trait and lesbianism as they are between a boy's sissiness and homosexuality. For this reason, lesbian girls are not nearly as likely to perceive themselves as different from their peers. This realization usually comes much later.

There are several other reasons why women are often considerably slower to recognize their same-sex feelings than men. One of these reasons is purely physiological. When a man has an erection he knows something has aroused him sexually. A woman does not have the same barometer of her sexual feelings, which are more diffuse. She can easily explain these responses to herself (if she even allows herself to be aware of them) as, for example, sisterly feelings, natural best-friend feelings, or admiration for a teacher, an older cousin, a female boss. Even if the girl or young woman is vaguely conscious that she is somehow different, often she is not aware of any sexual feelings in connection with this difference.

As a girl is growing up she is apt to be isolated if she does not date. So—she dates. Until recently, a woman's goal almost automatically was marriage. (If you had forgotten this fact, watch some of the old movies on television.) In the past it has been—and often still is—easy for a lesbian to marry, not realizing where her true primary emotional and sexual fulfillment lies. Sometimes a woman who is a lesbian engages in promiscuous heterosexual behavior, consciously or unconsciously hoping to find the right man, who never appears.

The heterosexual behavior of a woman who is lesbian

can be confusing to her parents. How can they know that the heterosexual behavior is really a cover-up or a denial of their daughter's same-sex feelings? The daughter herself may not yet know, or she may be struggling by herself with her same-sex feelings. She is not likely to confide this kind of thing to her parents at this stage of her life, particularly if she has not yet dared to confide it to herself.

Some women who are really lesbians believe they are asexual and even incapable of experiencing love because men do not interest them. One woman I know, until she was twenty-five, believed she was asexual. Then she recognized that she had strong feelings for a woman, feelings unlike anything she had ever experienced before. She was confused until she read *Lesbian/Woman*, by Del Martin and Phyllis Lyon.[4] As she read she saw herself in the book. "Oh, that's me, that's me!" she kept saying. "I can really feel!"[5]

For all the above reasons the emergence stage is likely to occur later for lesbians than for gay men.

One aspect of the emergence stage applies equally to gay men and lesbians: It is possible for both men and women to have many emotional and/or sexual encounters with persons of the same sex, sometimes over a period of years, and still not comprehend that they are gay or lesbian. The human mind has a marvelous capacity to block out much that it does not care to acknowledge. The lesbians or gay men either do not see themselves as matching the lesbian or gay stereotypes or they simply do not make the necessary connections between their behavior and the popular derogatory definitions of lesbianism or gayness.

In addition, same-sex-oriented people have heard and believed most of the erroneous platitudes society has developed concerning homosexuality:

"All children go through a phase when they have attachments to the same sex, but they outgrow this."

"You can choose who you want to be."

"Homosexuals are sick."

"Queers (dykes) should be shot."

"All things are possible through prayer."

And, with an unintentional play on words, "Therapy will straighten you out."

None of these statements is likely to help a gay man or lesbian come to grips with his or her orientation. They either encourage the person to believe that what he or she is feeling is transient and will change or they fill the same-sex-oriented person with such dread that it is easy to deny what otherwise might be apparent.

Acknowledgment

In the case of gay men the acknowledgment of emotional and sexual attraction to others of the same sex typically begins at puberty. There can be wide variation, however; some boys know from late childhood on that they are gay, whereas some men do not allow themselves this realization until the middle years of adulthood.

How does a person deal with the knowledge that he is gay or she is lesbian?

One way, as said earlier, is to pretend that these lesbian or gay feelings do not exist. Some same-sex-oriented people work hard at manufacturing heterosexual personalities. (Much of this, if not all, is done on an unconscious level.) They apply themselves diligently to learning the correct behavior demanded of them as would-be heterosexual persons. And for a time this may work.

In addition, the same-sex-oriented person often retreats from close involvement with anyone—family, friends, peers, teachers, co-workers. She or he is acting a role, and the fear of slipping and revealing her or his real thinking is always there. Every word that is said must be considered and screened before being uttered. "We did so-and-so" must be changed to "I did so-and-so"—an example of the monitoring that must go on every day, endlessly, if the facade is to be maintained. During this time of his or her life the same-sex-oriented person exists in a pervasive cloud of fear before the ever-present possibility of revealing his or her true self through an inadvertent slip of the tongue.

Almost always some situation occurs that causes this carefully constructed life and personality to come apart at the seams. Either the person begins, in one way or another, to break out of the psychic cage she or he has constructed or the continual stress of trying to be someone she or he is not takes a physical toll.

For instance, one married man spent many years being treated for high blood pressure, impotence, bleeding ulcers, and migraine headaches. Then, when the man was fifty, his physician happened to attend a sexuality workshop, where something clicked into place for the physician in relation to his patient. He returned from the workshop and asked the man point-blank if he was homosexual. Even though the patient had never had a homosexual experience, he admitted that his sexual fantasies had always involved men. He was terrified even to talk about his gay feelings but finally acknowledged that he had always denied them. Whether physical or psychic, the cost of denying one's real feelings, one's real self, is always high.

In years past, many doctors, mental health professionals (who might have been expected to know better), and religious counselors have suggested that the way for a man to overcome unwanted homosexual feelings was to find a nice girl and marry her. In conservative Christian circles this "remedy" is still commonly applied. Those familiar with the gay community know that this "cure" seldom works. They know that a good marriage is not built on such a basis, that the woman is demeaned by being used as a means to an end, and that if there are children, the accumulation of anguish that is stored up over the years for all concerned is astronomically increased. Knowingly or unknowingly, many lesbians have also taken the route of marriage either because they believed the right man would make them forget their attachments to other women or because they had no idea men could not provide the deep emotional and sexual fulfillment they needed.

In general, lesbians are less likely to seek counsel and help for their same-sex orientation than gay men, probably because it is easier for a woman to hide her sexual feelings from herself than it is for a man. Besides, lesbians are first of all women, and therefore, as women, they have been subtly programmed to see themselves as second-class citizens, to endure rather than to make waves, and to turn their aggressions in on themselves. For this reason they have often adopted self-destructive means of dealing with their inner pain. Alcohol and drug abuse are two avenues many lesbians have taken as refuges from their real feelings, or they have chosen to remain in bad marriages to atone for the guilt they feel at the breakdown of the marriage.

Another method of dealing with one's lesbian or gay feelings is rationalization, or bargaining. The teenager in junior or senior high school, the young adult in college or on the job who has not yet come out to others hears people talk about queers, faggots, homos, amazons, lezzies, and dykes, knowing deep inside they are talking about him or her. Is it surprising that at this point many same-sex-oriented people panic, feeling as if the name-callers had looked right through them, as if their souls had been laid bare for all to see? Overcome with shame, they ask themselves, "Do I really have all those horrible characteristics?" And they begin to set up tests for themselves. Many of these tests or bargains are not consciously perceived. They are more like reflex actions that, if successfully carried out, automatically prove a point never clearly articulated.

For a gay man, the tests may go like this:

"If I'm a good student, I'm not gay."
"If I'm a good athlete, I'm not gay."
"If I date women, I'm not gay."
"If I'm a good Christian, I'm not gay."
"If I fool around with men only when I'm drunk, I'm not gay."
"If I work twelve hours a day, I'm not gay."
"If I marry and have children, I'm certainly not gay."
"If I'm really, *really* macho, how can I possibly be gay?"

The lesbian counterpart of these tests might include:

"If I'm a good student, I'm not lesbian."
"If I date men, I'm not lesbian."
"If I'm a good Christian, I'm not lesbian."
"If I sleep with a lot of men, I certainly can't be lesbian."
"If I marry and have children, I can't possibly be lesbian."

One of the most desperate bargains for men is, "If I beat up gay people, obviously I'm not gay." Because society has not approved of women using physical violence as the answer to their problems, women are more apt to take out their fear of their own sexual selves in other ways. For example, in the military services a lesbian may deflect suspicion from herself by joining wholeheartedly in a lesbian witchhunt. "If I expose a lot of women as lesbians, I'm certainly not a lesbian."

There are other ways in which same-sex-oriented persons try to deal with their sexual orientation during the acknowledgment stage of their development. One of these may be a search for a deeper religious experience in the hope that God can "cure" the person's homosexuality. Another may be depression and/or withdrawal from society.

Most gay men and lesbians make the first disclosure of themselves to another person during the acknowledgment stage. This takes courage. Suppose the confidant turns away in disgust. Suppose he or she says that the same-sex-oriented person is bad, sinful, or unlovable because of who he or she is.

Until recently, society has not provided a place in which young people are safe to explore their sexuality in a helpful, nonthreatening way. Ideally, this exploration should take place in the home. Children and young people should be able to discuss freely with their parents any and all sexual matters and to receive wise and helpful guidance and education in formulating their values. Almost every parent knows that this is a utopian dream. The church, the school, and such groups as the Boy Scouts and Girl Scouts may also provide settings in which young people have more or less opportunity to explore their sexuality with the guidance of adults. In most cases the sexuality that is explored is heterosexuality.

Where can young people go to explore their suspected homosexuality and be dealt with understandingly, caringly, and nonjudgmentally? For many young people there are no such places. All they can do is struggle by themselves with the grim information society has given them about homosexuality and reach out tentatively to whoever promises help and understanding.

That the gay or lesbian person has verbalized his or her sexual feelings to someone else may be a major breakthrough and may have opened the door to further disclosures to other people.

The emergence and acknowledgment periods may be dangerous times for lesbian and gay persons. The anger, sadness, and confusion—"What does all this mean?" or "Why me?"—that commonly accompany the beginning stages of realizing one's same-sex orientation can get twisted into anxiety and depression. Tragically, the intensity of these feelings sometimes reaches a suicidal level, and rather than face her or his real self, the same-sex-oriented person chooses to escape the crushing dilemma through death.

Gay Men and Crashing Out, or Exploration

The next two stages of the coming-out process—crashing out, or exploration, and first relationships—differ in some important aspects for gay men and lesbians. Let us look at the male pattern first. Because the lesbian counterpart of crashing out usually occurs after a first relationship, it is considered here in that context.

Normally, once a gay man has a clear idea that he is gay he starts frequenting gay bars, if there are bars available and he is the proper age. Where else can he meet other gay people and know that they are gay? There *are* gay religious organizations in some areas, as well as other gay groups—such as gay athletes and gay professionals—but he probably does not know about them. So, whether he is a drinker or not, most likely he heads for a gay bar.

His main objective at this point usually is to make up for lost time. His straight friends have been dating for years while he has wondered (suspected and dreaded to face) what was "wrong" with himself because he was not interested in dating girls. Or he may have dated but did not experience the same feelings about girls that his friends described.

And now at long last he has come into his own. He has found others who share his feelings. Is it any wonder he may go a little wild? Even if he is twenty-five or thirty or forty, well established in his career or vocation, dealing with all other aspects of his life on an adult level, he may find himself acting socially like an irresponsible teenager. "What's wrong with me?" he may wonder. "I seem to have lost my senses." This is not true; he is simply making up for the time when, chronologically, he should have been reacting in this way but could not.

A gay friend in his early thirties told me that for six months he was at the bar every night. "I *had* to go," he said. "I would almost go crazy if I couldn't get there." He hinted delicately that the point of going to the bar was a compulsion to pick up a bedmate for the night. "All of a sudden that ended," he continued. "It was over, done with. I couldn't believe that I had ever done what I'd done. I haven't been to the bar now for months."

I explained to him why he might have behaved so compulsively, that unconsciously he was making up for lost time in a typically male-prescribed way.

If your gay son is in this stage of coming out, you may be distressed by indications of what seems like promiscuity. What can you do about it?

First, recognize that the sexual morals you and I grew up with are, to a large extent, things of the past, whether we are looking at heterosexual behavior or homosexual behavior. Are you aware of the messages television and the movies send continually? When you and I were growing up the pressure to refrain from premarital sex was great. Nowadays the pressure is almost as great to be sexually active before marriage. (Not that older generations *did* always refrain, but they were not as frank and open about such activity.)

Add to this the fact that because the gay community has

existed outside the pale of society for centuries, it has developed its own behavior patterns. If you tell people often enough that they are immoral and no good because they are who they are, many of them are going to believe this. While straight society exerts pressure to uphold the institution of marriage, the gay and lesbian communities have no means of proclaiming a committed relationship that is recognized and supported by society. There are many more-or-less committed relationships within the gay and lesbian communities, and nowadays—through the influence of such groups as the Metropolitan Community Church, Evangelicals Concerned, and others—there is a movement toward honoring and supporting these relationships through such services as Holy Union. In the wider community, however, there is no ethical or legal support for such unions.

In addition, men have been socialized according to a double standard. A man is thought to be most masculine when he is a sexual tiger. Traditionally, he has been *supposed* to be the initiator, the pursuer. Traditionally, *he* has been the one who sees how far he can go, the woman who has had to hold the line and say, "This far and no farther." The double standard has usually been the norm for society.

In an all-male community where the men behave with other men according to the ways in which they have been socialized—and according to the newest ways popularized by the sexual revolution in the past ten or twenty years— absence of sexual interaction is not a strong feature of that community.

Because the religious community has often washed its hands of all same-sex-oriented persons—except perhaps those who are living celibate lives—it has also cut itself off from having any ethical input into lesbian and gay communities. One begins to understand why these communities have formulated their own values and why some of these values do not necessarily contribute to the development of the whole person. Lesbian communities are probably better able to foster the development of the whole person than gay male communities, largely because women have been socialized to be more nurturant, more intuitive, and less aggressive sexually.

There is another aspect of your son's crashing out stage. Because crashing out, or exploration, for gay men—no matter what their chronological age—is a stage comparable to heterosexual adolescence, this may have been—or may now be—a chaotic period of emotional highs and lows for your son. If he does not clearly understand what he is looking for in any given situation where he gathers with other gay men, or if he does not understand that he may be looking for intellectual, spiritual, or emotional intimacy rather than sexual intimacy, he may invest all his needs in sexual intimacy, thinking this will supply everything he is looking for. When it does not he may assume that sexual intimacy with the next person *will* provide these things. In this way sexual activity can become a compulsive cycle that never satisfies if he is unaware of what he is looking for and how to find it.

Many gay men *are* looking for something more than sex. A number of them have said to me, "Well, the sex is OK, but what I really like is when a man holds me close." All human beings have a need to be touched. The enthusiastic embracing that goes on in Lutheran, Episcopal, and Catholic gay communion services at the passing of the peace is perhaps one way of satisfying this hunger nonsexually.

Suppose you feel your son is too active sexually. What are you going to do about it? If he is an adult and you no longer have control over his life as you did (or thought you did) when he was growing up, is there anything you can do? If he is not yet legally an adult, what can you do?

You, as a parent, need not remain silent in either case.

What *is* of great importance is the manner in which you talk with your son about the sexual activity that concerns you. If you issue directions as an all-wise parent to a naughty child or dwell only on the evils (as you see them) of such behavior or state *your* feelings without taking time to listen to what he has to say, you are certain not to make any headway with your son. He will tune you out and erect a wall between himself and you.

In dealing with this situation be honest with yourself about your aim in talking with your son. Do you want to impose your values on him? Or do you want to *talk over* the situation as one adult to another, *exchange* ideas? *Talk over* and *exchange* mean that ideas are going in both directions. Listen (and I mean *listen, hear*— not simply be silent until it is your turn again to talk) as well as set forth your views. You *can* express your feelings, your puzzlement, your values, your need for clarification of the situation, your willingness to listen.

"I don't understand why you're being so active sexually," expresses your *feelings* rather than being a heavy-handed condemnation of your child. "It's different from my values."

You may think your feelings about your son's sexual activity are related to his gayness. Yet if you knew a straight son or daughter was very active sexually, you probably would feel the same way. Express these thoughts to your son, that you are not viewing this as a gay issue, but rather as an issue of general sexual values.

"I don't like what's going on," you can say. "I need to understand your values about sexual intimacy and what you really want out of such intimacy."

In talking with my children about sexual values and behaviors I have discovered the tremendous difference between the somewhat Victorian atmosphere in which I grew up and the increasingly permissive sexual climate in which they have come of age. I have discovered that they have difficulty envisioning the influences that shaped my values. For my part, I had greatly underestimated the prevailing influences with which society had surrounded them as they were growing up.

If your son is confusing emotional intimacy with sexual intimacy, talking it over with him (*not* arguing, *not* condemning) may open the door to a different perspective for him. If it does not, you may have begun to understand his viewpoint—even though you may not approve of it—and he may have gotten a new perspective on your values. The end product of your conversation(s) may not be agreement between the two of you, although that might seem to be the end you desired. Knowing that his parents have listened to him, have been honest about their thoughts and feelings, and have not tried to coerce him may have a powerful effect on your son, an effect you may not necessarily be aware of. Such an exchange says to your child, "The door is open between us. We can be honest with each other without always having to agree." It says, "You are an adult, responsible for your own life, and I care about you enough to allow you to be a person in your own right, not a parental appendage who must agree with me on every point."

Most important, by raising such issues you may have challenged him to search for new and more constructive values.

First Relationships, Lesbian and Gay

For gay males, the next stage in the coming-out process, after crashing out, is probably the development of a first relationship. For lesbians, the development of a first relationship usually occurs immediately after the acknowledgment stage.

Generally, a gay man seeks out the gay community on

acknowledging his sexual orientation. He may take some time getting around to his first relationship because he is so busy in the crashing out stage. Lesbians, on the contrary, are more apt to enter into a first relationship immediately after coming to terms with their sexual orientation. Often such relationships are formed in isolation from any type of lesbian community, with the first woman who responds to the new lesbian's need for relationship. The partner is not chosen for suitability from a number of eligible friends and acquaintances, because usually at this point in her life, no such group exists for the lesbian. She simply falls into a relationship with the first available woman.

Some of these couples remain together for years, even though the partners may be hopelessly mismatched. Often they have no contact with other lesbians. But society's emphasis on the desirability of permanence in relationships involving love and sex seems to influence women to remain in the bad relationship and to feel a deep sense of failure if they cannot make the relationship work. Even when lesbians *do* know other lesbians, society's pressure on women toward relationship building and the stronger link for women between sex and love are apt to move lesbians quickly and prematurely toward pairing off, joining their lives together and making commitments that should not be made so soon.

Sometimes there is a secondary reason for remaining in the relationship; this is true for gay men as well as for lesbians. Fear grips the partners: "If I break up this relationship, will I find someone else?" Having a poor relationship may be preferable to not having any relationship. Although some of these relationships do endure—whether they deserve to or not—many founder within a few years.

The end of a first relationship is as painful for a same-sex-oriented person as the breakup of a heterosexual first love affair (whether it has included sexual activity or not) or a marriage. If you want to be of real assistance to your child in a difficult period of her or his life, you will listen, you will acknowledge the grief and pain your child is experiencing, and you will withhold any condemnation. Heterosexual or homosexual, when a love relationship falls apart your child *hurts*.

You hope your child learns and grows from this experience. In all likelihood your son will move to the stage of self-definition and reintegration. Your daughter may also, or she may move on to the lesbian version of the crashing out stage.

Crashing Out, or Exploration, for Lesbians

Whether your lesbian daughter crashed out before she entered into a first relationship or after, she is less likely to have as many sexual encounters as a gay man, and the encounters will probably not be as impersonal. Because society has trained women to be more responsible for relationship building than are men, few lesbians are much interested in casual sexual encounters for any prolonged period.

Whether or not your daughter has been through a first relationship that foundered, in the crashing out stage she explores the possibilities for dating other women and finding a partner. If she has been through an unsatisfactory relationship, she may eventually *choose* another partner with more care and discrimination, rather than falling into the first alliance that becomes possible.

Also at this point your daughter's evolution may include involvement in the lesbian political, cultural, and social community, rather than involvement in many and promiscuous sexual encounters. This may mean joining a coming-out group, a lesbian softball team, or a lesbian chorus; hanging out at lesbian bars and coffeehouses; and in other ways expanding her connections to meet other women who may be available for friendships, dating, and relationships.

During the period of first relationships and crashing out many lesbians choose primarily women—and especially other lesbians—as friends. Most parents interpret this as isolationism or man-hating on the part of their lesbian daughters. "If she'd give herself a chance, she might find she liked men," the parents think. Or they believe other lesbians are out to get and brainwash their daughter.

What parents do not realize is that such exclusiveness is a way for the lesbian who is trying hard to find her way in new and unfamiliar territory to develop support in a generally hostile world. It is also a way for her to have comfortable social relationships, because many heterosexual persons are not comfortable with lesbians. Lesbians must guard their behavior in heterosexual public places. They may not hold hands as heterosexual couples do; nor may they dance together. For this reason lesbians feel freer and more at ease in lesbian places and seek these places in preference to those that are heterosexual.

The same is true of gay men. When they seek out gay friends and gay areas they are looking for support and the opportunity to be themselves. They have not been subverted or brainwashed, as many parents think.

Self-definition and Reintegration

The final stage of your homosexual child's development into a whole human being with a same-sex orientation is self-definition and reintegration. Your child, lesbian or gay, now has a variety of experiences as a same-sex-oriented person to serve as background material against which consciously to shape her or his life. Your child is also in a better position to evaluate goals, short and long term, and make informed and careful decisions about how public to be with her or his private self. Your child is ready to make these decisions in the light of a healthy self-interest, personal pride, and self-respect, rather than reacting out of fear, shame, and desperate need for approval or acceptance. And because life is a process of change, new situations will continue to provide challenges to your child in assessing the risks and benefits of sharing her or his lesbian or gay identity with others.

During the self-definition and reintegration stage—which is less a stage than an ongoing learning process—your child's life will expand much like any person's life expands, whether hetero- or homosexual. New feelings about oneself continue to emerge, and one learns to understand these feelings and integrate them into life.

Your child will find and explore new groups, new friends, and perhaps, of necessity, new primary relationships. Your child will return to the acknowledgment stage each time a decision is made to share her or his true identity with a family member, employer, colleague, or friend.

How can you, as a parent, help your child in this stage of change and growth? Do the same things you would for your heterosexual child. See him or her as a responsible, mature person. Respect his or her individual personhood. Everyone needs to be dealt with and appreciated as a unique person.

Coping with the Idea of Your Child's Lover

Suppose your child is in a primary relationship—in plain English, living with a lover. Many straight people—particularly parents—find the term *lover* distasteful. In the heterosexual world the word usually has a specialized meaning: a person with whom one is having a sexual relationship outside of marriage. The word thereby acquires a faintly disreputable tinge. "Why not use the word friend?" people ask, "or partner or companion?"

Looking at the terminology from the lesbian's or gay

man's point of view, one becomes aware of several things. The gay man or lesbian wants to indicate that a certain person is special to him or her. One has many friends, but this person is more than that. "Partner" sounds like a business partner; it conveys none of the real feelings surrounding the person. "Companion" has the connotation of friend—or of someone who cares for an elderly person—or a delicate way of indicating that here is an extracurricular diversion of a famous person. "Spouse," when used correctly, indicates that a legal marriage has taken place. Bishop Paul Moore's wife, rather imaginatively, used the term consort to denote those persons to whom her children were lovingly but not legally attached.[6] At the moment, however, there is no universally accepted term by which a gay man or a lesbian can say to the world, "This is the person with whom I am sharing my life in a loving, caring, genital relationship." Straight persons are proud to refer to "my husband," "my wife," or, if the couple is feminist-oriented, "my spouse." Why should not same-sex-oriented persons also proclaim to the world at large their love relationship?

But suppose the thought of your son or daughter having sexual activity with a person of the same sex is utterly abhorrent to you. The idea of a lover may be even worse. Perhaps the thought of sexual activity outside of marriage would be bad enough for you to cope with in a heterosexual child, but in a same-sex-oriented child it seems impossible that you could come to terms with the idea. "Why can't they just be friends?" you wonder. Things would be so much easier.

Many parents refuse to deal with a child's lover. "You can come home, but not your 'friend,'" they say. They would not think of saying to a married daughter or son, "*You* may come home, but don't bring your husband (wife)." In your child's eyes the lover occupies the same relationship to you as the spouse in a heterosexual situation. You may not see it this way. If you do not accept the lover, you are likely to lose more than you gain, because you have thereby weakened your relationship with your child.

Perhaps you have difficulty accepting your child's lover because of the fantasy pictures your mind paints about how people of the same sex "do it." These pictures may be so repellent to you that you do not want anything to do with your child's lover. You may feel the lover has seduced your child. This may be especially true if your son or daughter is young and the lover is much older.

If this is the case, perhaps you should discover the source of your discomfort. The general idea that the nitty-gritty of homosexual sex is abhorrent to you because it is "unnatural" may be covering up feelings you are unaware of. Psychologically, it is untrue that what you do not know cannot hurt you. What is buried in your unconscious can be detrimental to your peace of mind and well-being.

Begin by going back over your sexual autobiography. What ideas about sex were inculcated in you as a child? What ideas did you absorb from your parents and the other adults who surrounded you? What ideas did you absorb from your peers? What were your childhood and adolescent sexual fantasies? What were your childhood and adolescent sexual experiences? How did you feel about these experiences, or the lack of them, at the time? If such introspection generates an undue amount of fear, shame, and distress, you may want to seek counseling in dealing with your own sexuality.

"But I was getting along just fine with my sexuality until this happned," you may be thinking. "Why should *I* go for counseling when it's my child's 'unnatural' sex that is at fault? Let *him (her)* get the counseling."

True, you may have been getting along fine until you

learned of your child's homosexuality. Now the whole equation of your life has changed. This is not your child's fault; nor is it yours. No one is at fault. New information—your child's same-sex orientation—has come into your life, and you cannot cope with it. This hurts you and your relationship with your child. Either you curtail or cut off the relationship with your child or you take steps to grow in order that you may maintain a loving and noncondemning relationship with your child. Making your child choose between you and her or his partner can only result in hurt for everyone.

You may feel your child has hurt you deeply. You may be in deep pain because of your child's same-sex orientation, especially as you come face to face with the outward manifestation of this orientation—your child's lover.

The pain is *yours,* and you cannot deal with *your* pain by trying to change someone else. You can deal with this pain only by exploring its dimensions, only by heading into it and through it to the other side. There are no bypasses around pain. When one tries to bypass it one finds it waiting up ahead, and in the meantime it has become more formidable, having "earned interest," so to speak, along the way.

Some people can head into their pain and work through it by themselves. Others need help—a wise friend, an understanding doctor or minister. If such a helper is not available to you, search out a professional mental health counselor to serve as a sounding board and to offer guidance as you plow through this painful territory.

If you are to understand your child and his or her relationship with a lover, there are some things it might be helpful for you to know. First, the problems your child and his or her lover may face are most likely to be of the human variety rather than specifically gay or lesbian problems.

Your son's or daughter's first relationship may be fragile. Often lesbians and gay men enter into relationships before they are ready for such experiences. The miracle of being in love has burst on them. They desperately want to find persons with whom they can share their whole selves. Possibly, they have been so starved for love from persons of the same sex that they latch onto the first ones who offer themselves. This is the love of the century, they think, not realizing they may be in love with love rather than with a lover.

What is going on between your child and the lover is not so different from what happens in millions of heterosexual relationships. Often the dynamics of the relationship between the two partners could just as well go on between heterosexual partners.

Let us expand this idea. The same dynamics can occur between brothers and/or sisters or even between two unrelated people who decide to live together in a nonsexual relationship. The situation of an unmarried friend opened my eyes to this fact. Her parents had died, leaving her and an unmarried sister to share the family home. As time went on it became apparent to my friend that she could not live with her sister and avoid a nervous breakdown. One of the most difficult tasks she ever faced was to tell her sister she was moving out and then actually move.

The facet of her story that interested me the most was that the problems within the relationship between her and her sister almost duplicated some of the problems that had caused my divorce. Although there was no sexual aspect to her and her sister's relationship, the similarity in other respects between her situation and mine was uncanny. Right then I realized that a large percentage of problems in marriage and in living-together relationships have no connection with sex. They are interpersonal problems that can occur in any relationship where two (or more) people occupy the same living quarters. If there is a sexual aspect to the relationship, the strains may be evidenced in sexual as well as other ways. But most of the stresses do not originate in the sexual connection; they originate in the human connection that occurs when people share living space.

For most of her or his life your same-sex-oriented child has had to cope with society's hostile evaluation. Every day your child must cope with misunderstanding and discrimination. Perhaps you can begin to recognize how important it is for you, as a parent, to obtain accurate information about homosexuality and to continue to love your lesbian or gay child. She or he has enough difficulties to contend with in everyday life, difficulties resulting not from a willful choice or from bad parenting but from the circumstances life has handed her or him—and you.

This is why it is so important for you to make the effort to understand your child and your child's sexual orientation. It is natural for you to be upset, to fall back on the ideas and beliefs about homosexuality with which you grew up. These beliefs and ideas have collided with the information that your child is same-sex-oriented, and this collision is causing you to experience pain, disorientation, a sense of loss, and grief.

Can you deal with the intense feelings your child's coming out has aroused in you? Will you be able to reconcile all the different feelings you are experiencing? Is it worthwhile making the effort to accept (not necessarily approve) your child's sexuality and maintain a close and caring relationship with her or him?

Each person's answer, of course, will be different. But thousands of parents *have* made the effort and have found it more worthwhile than they believed possible.

Nobody—or almost nobody—says it is easy. Occasionally, I talk with a parent to whom his or her child's homosexuality presented no particular problem. Most parents, however, have considerable difficulty dealing with the same-sex orientation of their children. Perhaps a glimpse at some of the dynamics of parenting will help you understand why this is so and will offer a way of living with this fact of your life.

Chapter 7

Letting Go

Tom Braden, a newspaper columnist, has captured the essence of changes in family relationships that come as the children in the family grow up.[1] He first became aware of the change after his children had returned to college from a Thanksgiving vacation. During their stay at home he began to realize that he was no longer the final source of authoritative information for his children. He discovered that when his "facts" were tested against "facts" given by other people, his turned out to be "what people 'used' to think."

He also discovered that, as father, he no longer controlled his children. One evening after dinner the children, both male and female, went out. They didn't ask permission, nor could he recall afterward that they had even bothered to tell him they were going. They simply went. One of them, without calling home, spent the night at a friend's house. He had had a few beers with his friend Bill and decided to stay all night. A year or two before, Braden says, this could not have happened, or if it had, there would have been a family row about it. Now the son is 21 and, Braden writes, "he knows I disapprove. I wonder whether I should disapprove."

Braden concludes the column with the question: "Why didn't somebody tell me that there would come a time when I would be stripped of my powers and when the word 'father' would mean not much more than 'old friend'?"

Mothers also face pitfalls as their children mature. At age eighty-two Florida Scott-Maxwell, an author, dramatist, and analytical psychologist, wrote with great insight about the unconscious feelings that cause mothers to react in seemingly odd ways:

A mother's love for her children, even her inability to let them be, is because she is under a painful law that the life that passed through her must be brought to fruition. Even when she swallows it whole she is only acting like any frightened mother cat eating its young to keep it safe. It is not easy to give closeness and freedom, safety plus danger.

No matter how old a mother is she watches her middle-aged children for signs of improvement. It could not be otherwise for she is impelled to know that the seeds of value sown in her have been winnowed. She never outgrows the burden of love, and to the end she carries the weight of hope for those she bore. Oddly, very oddly, she is forever surprised and even faintly wronged that her sons and daughters are just people, for many mothers hope and half expect that their new-born child will make the world better, will somehow be a redeemer.[2]

Nobody sets out to be a mother or father who smothers. We may have the best intentions in the world of being marvelous parents, but somehow along the way something trips us up. Or we may have assumed that knowing how to be a mother or father is an instinctive skill that surfaces when the baby is born. Birds and dogs and horses and cats know how to be parents—or at least mothers. But we are not birds or animals, and therefore, we have considerably different mental equipment. The instincts that enable nonhuman living creatures to survive by doing what comes naturally, without conscious thought, do not operate in human beings within the same restrictive limits. True, we do carry within us some ideas of how to be parents. But a great deal of our human action depends on how we learn to act.

We learn to be parents in a number of ways. One is by imitation of our parents. If we had good parents, we have a head start on our own parenting. If we had examples of deficient parenting as we grew up—abusing parents, to cite a glaring example—we are more likely to become deficient parents ourselves than we otherwise might.

We also learn a great deal about being a father or a mother by what society tells us a father or a mother should be. Much of our learning is unconscious. We absorb by osmosis, from the air around us, ideas of how a mother or a father behaves. We are not even conscious that we are receiving and retaining these ideas. Often when we become parents we act in certain ways without knowing why.

In addition, the particular culture in which we grow up influences our actions. The ideal Victorian mother would behave totally differently from the ideal mother of the 1980s. An aboriginal mother would behave quite differently from a mother in a civilized Western culture.

One of the ideas about motherhood acquired from the culture around us is the feeling that a mother's love is instinctive, unquestioning, and total. In the beginning a baby is almost helpless. The mother does everything for the child without asking anything in return. Because of this, mother love is considered to be the most sacred of all emotional bonds.

What have not been so well publicized are other important aspects of a mother's love. During the first months and years of a child's life a mother gives and gives and then gives some more. We forget that the essence of a mother's love, as Erich Fromm has pointed out, is

to care for the child's *growth,* and that means *to want the child's separation from herself.* . . . The mother must not only tolerate, she must wish and support the child's separation. It is only at this stage that motherly love becomes such a difficult task, that it requires unselfishness, the ability to give everything and to want nothing but the happiness of the loved one.[3]

Note that in the beginning the mother's unselfishness demands that she do everything for her child. The time comes, however, when her "unselfishness, the ability to give everything and to want nothing," no longer means the total immersion in her child that unselfishness meant in the child's early years. Now the unselfishness means that she lets go, withdraws, no longer tries to control and direct.

For a mother to want this separation of the child from herself is not always easy, although I believe it is easier for some women than for others. Some mothers find the helpless-baby stage more endearing and rewarding than their children's older stages, and for these women it may be more difficult to want their children to be separated from them. This may be why some women look forward so longingly to grandchildren.

Personally, I have had the opposite difficulty. I had never been around young children and was not comfortable with the baby stage. I looked forward almost desperately sometimes to the day when I could relate to my children in more adult ways. I was ashamed that I was not more enthusiastic about my children as helpless little bundles, toddlers, and preschoolers. Something must be wrong with me, I thought, until one day I discovered that a friend, the mother of *six* teenage and young adult children, had had the same feelings. "Oh, I enjoyed my children much more when they started to grow up than when they were babies," she said—and a load rolled off my mind.

It is not always easy to know how to shift gears in parent/child relationships as our children grow. We may not recognize that we are still smothering our children. It may be painful suddenly to discover that our children are making their own decisions without even telling us what these decisions are. But presumably, this is what fathers and mothers have been aiming for all along.

A father's love, according to Fromm, "should give the growing child an increasing sense of competence and eventually permit him to become his own authority and to dispense with that of father."[4]

That it may be no easier for a father to let go than for a mother is evident from what Braden writes. Certainly it is difficult to be demoted from the position of father, the source of wisdom and authority, to not much more than the position of old friend. And yet how fortunate if a father can in fact become an old friend to his children. Perhaps this is the basic goal toward which we, as parents—father or mother—need to aim as our children grow up. No longer are we the commanders, the authorities, the people without whom our children would have difficulty surviving. The parent/child relationship must become much more that of good friends—adult to adult—and rich are the rewards if such a relationship of mutual respect and mutual caring can be achieved.

It is not only we parents, however, who may have difficulty making the transition from a parent/child relationship to an adult/adult relationship.[5] From the moment of birth and for many years thereafter our children have been dependent on us for care and sustenance. Unconsciously, they have come to perceive us as powerful persons. As mother or father, we govern, modulate, and control almost everything that happens to our children in their early years.

As our children mature, they continue to carry, deep within, an unconscious perception of us as "big" (powerful) and of themselves as "little" (powerless). The conscious mind knows this is not an accurate perception. Yet unconscious ideas exert great power, a fact of which we are all frequently unaware.

Even though our children may now be adults they may continue to relate to us as if we were still the directors, the caretakers. Within our children may still be a residue of the child-to-parent relationship rather than an adult-to-adult relationship. Often a conscious effort is necessary on the part of one or both sides to move out of the parent/child habit patterns into adult-to-adult patterns.

What is an adult-to-adult pattern? How can we relate to our children, how can our children relate to us, in an adult mode without sacrificing love and caring? Can it be done?

Florida Scott-Maxwell, expressing herself as a mother, writes: "I have learned the hard truth a mother learns slowly, that the quick of intimacy she has known becomes hope for loved strangers."[6]

Erich Fromm, speaking more dispassionately, characterizes mature love as "union under the condition of preserving one's integrity, one's individuality."[7]

How can one define the union Fromm speaks of? To me, the word caring could replace union and the sentence would mean the same thing. "Mature love is *caring* under the condition of preserving one's integrity, one's individuality."

The extreme importance of these last two conditions—

preserving one's integrity, one's individuality—was graphically illustrated to me a number of years ago. I was attending an open-ended Christian therapy group with friends. At one point during the session a middle-aged woman, with tears running down her cheeks, said she was experiencing great pain and difficulty in her life, because often when she passed strangers on the street she felt a desperate hate for them.

"What's wrong with me?" she sobbed out. "How can I hate them? I don't even know them!" That she was a Christian and therefore felt under a moral imperative to love rather than hate brother and sister human beings contributed to her distress.

I looked closely at this woman. She wore a shapeless, nondescript tweed suit. A button was missing from her suit jacket and the bottom of her skirt sagged on one side where the hem had come loose. Her hair was pulled untidily into a knot on top of her head, and she wore no makeup or jewelry. Her stockings were wrinkled about her ankles, and her shoes were "sensible" and homely.

"Who is she?" I whispered to my neighbor.

"You won't believe this," my neighbor whispered back, "but she is the head of the research department of a large corporation. She is a brilliant, capable woman," he continued, "but she lives at home with her parents and they treat her like a four-year-old."

It was suddenly clear to me why this woman "hated" strangers. The impossible role demanded of her at home had resulted in a tremendous amount of hatred and anger within her toward her parents. Her inability to free herself from her parents' domination had also resulted in overwhelming anger and hatred toward herself, hence her careless appearance. Apparently, she did not think she was worth fussing over. Because she seemingly did not dare to face and deal with her unacceptable feelings, she was unconsciously projecting her anger and hatred onto strangers, rather than dealing with her feelings and her circumstances more maturely and rationally.

This is an extreme example of what can happen when we do not allow our children to grow up, when we do not thrust them more and more out of the psychological nest. It does, however, point up the fact that once a person has reached maturity agewise, she or he has also passed a psychological and spiritual checkpoint in life. As parents, we cannot choose whether or not we want to allow our children to pass this checkpoint, just as we cannot choose whether or not we want to let our babies grow physically out of babyhood or our children out of childhood. This is something that happens, and there is no stemming the tide. Neither do our children have any choice in the matter of growing up into adulthood. Peter Pan may have successfully managed to escape maturity, but no one else has been able to pull it off.

If we try to keep our children under our authority after they have reached the late teens, we are severely crippling them in their ability to deal with life. If, as emerging adults, they cannot make their own choices and decisions, even though these may be at variance with our wishes, a great deal of pain and difficulty is likely to await them five, ten, or twenty years in the future.

It seems part of the very structure of life that if a grown man or woman allows himself or herself to be dominated by one or both parents, he or she will end up hating both parents and self. It does not matter whether the adult child has clung to the domination of the parents or has inwardly rebelled against it, even though allowing the domination to continue. The result is the same. Something deep within the center of each person knows instinctively that the psychological umbilical cord to the parents must be cut. If this separation does not take place, the child becomes emotionally crippled to a greater or lesser extent.

If a relationship of mature caring between parents and

child is to exist, there first has to be some sort of psychic separation, a letting go on both sides, a learning to live independently of the other. The paradox of real closeness between two persons lies in the ability of each to exist independently of the other. Only as grown children learn to exist independently of their parents and the parents of their grown children can each side be free to care about the other, to allow the other person to have his or her own feelings and not be too threatened by these feelings.

Up to now everything in this chapter applies with equal force to *any* adult child and his or her parents, not only to those family groups where one member is oriented toward same-sex relationships. Too often both parents and lesbian or gay children think, "If it weren't for the homosexual factor in our family, we would not have to deal with these problems of relationships."

Of course this is not true. The problem does not arise because one family member has a different sexual orientation. The same problem exists in families where all the children are heterosexual. It arises because the family is a community of human beings who must grow and change through the various stages in the lives of both parents and children.

There *is* one particular problem you as a lesbian or gay child must face that your straight sisters and brothers are not called on to cope with. Chapter 6 deals with your public self versus your private self, and chapter 4, with the fact that, as you were growing up, your mother and father parented only your public self. You lived with an unspoken fear: "If they knew who I really was, would they still love me?" The person for whom your parents did things was a false self. Their care of you, their concern, their guidance, their support materially and emotionally, their understanding of you, their affirmation of you—all these things were given to the boy or girl, young man or young woman whom you were impersonating; they were not given to the real you.

Part of the reason you have come out to your parents may be that you still want and need most of these things from them, and unconsciously—or perhaps consciously—you are hoping your parents hear your cry of need and respond. Even if you have reached the age where you no longer need their physical care, their guidance, and their material support, you may still long for their concern about you, their emotional caring and support of you, their understanding, their affirmation of the person you really are.

Right here may be the crux of the matter for you and for your parents. You may be crying desperately to them, "Mother, Dad, please, *please, PLEASE* love me as I am." And they may be crying back to you just as desperately, "You have threatened my inmost self so strongly that I can't love the gay or lesbian you."

What can you, as a son or daughter—what can you, as parents—do in the face of such an impasse?

This book attempts to help you, both parents and children, discover what can be done. The resolution of the problem boils down to several things: being patient (time often *does* help, at least to an extent); coming to a new and deeper understanding of yourself, whether children or parents, because you cannot reach out to others if you do not understand yourself; struggling toward mature forms of love and caring.

But suppose, as parents, you cannot give what your child wants. Your values are too deeply embedded for you to change. How far *can* you go with your child? What *can* you offer? Can you at least say, "I want to keep in touch with you. I want to know about your job or your career. For the present I don't want to talk about your lesbianism (gayness), but I'd like to keep the door at least ajar between us"? Can you go this far? Can you be frank with your child about the limitations of what you can handle? I have found in dealing with my children that if I am honest with them about my real feelings, they can handle that much better than if I try to pretend I am feeling something I am not. My pretense puts a distance between us. It says, "This is something we daren't touch or talk about." To breach this kind of silence later is difficult.

What you cannot do is ask your child to change so you will be comfortable. You may want your child to live a celibate life, or you may want him or her to become heterosexual. Psychologically, one cannot make oneself comfortable at the expense of another person without in some way destroying a part of the other person.

Looking at the impasse from the other side, what will you, as the gay or lesbian child, do if your parents cannot accept your sexual orientation?

You will have to learn to accept your parents as *they* are. This is not easy. And it happens to many children in many different situations that have nothing to do with sexuality, so you are not alone—for whatever this is worth to you. As I stated earlier, I spent at least thirty years trying to change my mother before I finally realized that I had to accept her as she was and do whatever was necessary to protect myself from her desire to dominate me—which she tried to do even at a distance of a thousand miles!

What can you do in order to live with the situation? You may need to allow yourself to experience all the grief and rejection you are trying to avoid. In this effort you may find considerable help in the chapter "Finishing," in Judy Tatelbaum's book *The Courage to Grieve*.[8] You deal with the situation by working with yourself, or you may need some help from a trained counselor. Whatever else you do, *do not* put your feelings aside, thinking they will go away if you pay no attention to them. You can play ostrich for fifty years, providing you do not have a nervous breakdown or develop ulcers, arthritis, or some other physical outworking of your pain that forces you to confront the psychological pain. When you pull your head out of the sand the pain will be right there, as fresh and as agonizing as it was fifty years earlier. You may as well work it through now and then get on with living.

Some lesbian and gay people, as well as some parents, terminate the parent/child relationship. A number of parents have done this, but I know of only one same-sex-oriented person who has terminated the relationship with his family—not because they could not accept his sexual orientation (he has not come out to them), but because other aspects of the relationship were so hurtful to him he could not remain in the relationship. Perhaps other children have separated themselves from their parents because of the way the parents were dealing, or not dealing, with the same-sex orientation.

I am filled with the hope that, as a parent, you can accept the person your child really is. "Accept" does not necessarily mean "approve." No parent approves of everything his or her child does, and no child approves of everything his or her parents do.

Coming back to the definition of mature love, can you *care* about the other while still leaving him or her, parent or child, free to be himself or herself? As a grown child, you cannot "go home again" in the sense of returning to emotional dependence on your parents. If you try it, you end up hating yourself and your parents. As parents of a grown child, you cannot keep your child in the same dependent relationship that existed during his or her growing-up years.

Again, this does not mean parents and grown children cannot maintain warm relationships with each other. This does not mean grown children cannot talk over things with parents and get the parents' ideas and perspective on a job change, a proposed move, investment of money, or anything else. Happy are the adult children who have parents to whom they can go for advice and counsel, knowing that the parents will share what wisdom they may have on the subject and yet not try to coerce their children into something they do not want to do. Happy are the parents whose children feel comfortable turning to them—as well as to other adults, both peers and older friends—to talk over a matter that is important in their lives.

Happy also are the parents who can turn to their children and talk over their—the parents'—problems and decisions. Personally, I find it a continuing joy to be able to go to my children and discuss my concerns with them. I appreciate their listening and offering their ideas, even though I may not always take their advice or suggestions, just as they do not always take mine. It is exciting to me that the babies I nurtured and raised are now responsible people with whom I can have adult-to-adult interchange.

Real togetherness comes not from coercion. Rather, it can grow only in the soil of the freedom that comes from letting go of the other person. We, as human beings—parent or child—cannot ultimately satisfy our deepest needs through relationship to another person, no matter who this person is—child, parent, spouse, significant other, friend, mentor, therapist. We can satisfy our deepest needs only by being in touch with our deepest selves. It is out of our deepest selves that we discover the strength to give, to love, in a nondemanding way.

Letting go of parents by adult children and of adult children by parents is therefore not a destruction, an ending. Rather, it is a creative rearrangement of relationships that promises new and satisfying associations between parents and children. One of the marvelous facts of life is that every ending carries within itself the potential for a new beginning.

Chapter 8

Parents Also Come Out

Several years ago I visited my hometown. I was in the process of finding a publisher for my book *My Son Eric* and realized that if the manuscript were accepted for publication, it would only be a matter of time before my friends there learned that my son is gay. Before I went I decided, with Eric's approval, that whenever the opportunity arose I would say that Eric is gay.

The experiment provided me with some interesting insights. Mainly, I discovered that most people did not want to talk with me about my son's being gay. It seemed to be an uncomfortable topic for them. *I* may have been ready to talk about it, but they were unprepared to deal with the subject on such short notice.

In looking back on this experience I realize that, because of my desire to come out as the parent of a gay child, sometimes I may have introduced the subject inappropriately. Another side of the matter is that if one waited to come out until people were ready to receive the information, there would seldom be any coming out.

The last thing you may want to do at this point is come out to *anyone* as the parent of a lesbian or gay child. Or, the matter of your parental coming out may not be a big problem for you—but in that case you are probably not reading this book.

"Do I *have* to come out as the parent of a gay or lesbian child?" you may be wondering. "Can't I go through life without saying anything about this to anyone?"

To make things more difficult, your child may not understand why you do not want to acknowledge to others that your son is gay or your daughter is a lesbian, and he or she may be eager to push you toward such an open acknowledgment. If each of you has some understanding of the conflicting dynamics in the situation, this understanding may help you resolve the tension between you.

A parent's thoughts are apt to run something like this: "What will *my* parents, my brothers and sisters, my other relatives, my friends, my minister or priest or rabbi, my co-workers think about me? They'll think I was a bad parent, that I did something wrong in raising my child. They'll think there is something wrong with my marriage, that it's a failure. Maybe they're right about all these things. I must have failed somewhere along the line or this wouldn't have happened."

The more unsure you are about yourself as a person or as a parent, the more terrifying may be the thought of standing revealed before others as the father or mother of a same-sex-oriented child. This is not merely an impersonal fact you are considering passing on. This is information that could confirm others' suspicions that you are an inadequate person, a stupid or a bad person, even a dismal failure. You may not be conscious of any of this, much less be able to express it. All you know is that *at all costs* this information about your child must be kept secret.

To your son or daughter, however, this need for secrecy may seem like betrayal. "My parents are ashamed of me. They are denying before our relatives and friends the person I really am. If my parents really loved me, they would let people know I'm lesbian (gay)."

When these two sets of attitudes meet, a collision is bound to result. To make matters more difficult, maybe neither side can express what each is really feeling. You, as parents, know only that your child is trying to force you to do something you are determined not to do, and your child knows only that you are being stubborn about something that is absolutely necessary to him or her. Each feels that the other "can't possibly love me or she or he (they) would do what I (we) ask."

Impasses like this are hard to break; being honest about one's deep inner feelings is not easy. Only when one is willing to endure the pain of expressing one's fears, when one musters the courage to do this can any progress be made.

If you, as parents, could dare to verbalize your fears that your child's same-sex orientation results from your failure as parents, you would open the way to discovering that this is a false belief, that you are torturing yourselves needlessly. If your child could express the rejection she or he is feeling because of your refusal to tell others, you would at least have the opportunity to reassure your child that you love her or him and to ask for patience until you, too, are ready to come out. You could remind your child that it probably took her or him a while to decide to come out to others.

If you, as parents, do decide you are ready to come out, another question presents itself: "May I give this information about my child to anyone I want or should I check with my child first?"

No one answer applies to all situations. It is important to work out with your child both your and your child's real feelings in each particular situation. Whom do you want to tell or not tell? Why? Whom does your child want to tell or not tell? Why? Both you and your child may have to bring all your love, forbearance, courtesy, and patience to these discussions, as well as honesty about what each of you is really feeling. These discussions may be times of tension, but the tension can be constructive if both parties remember that words can wound, and strive to control tempers. "*I* feel pressured (threatened, unhappy, scared)" is always better than "*You* don't understand (care, love me)."

Tense as such discussions may get, they can result in greater understanding on both sides. They may not always result in complete satisfaction for you and your child. Almost by definition, family situations demand concession and compromise.

To understand why you do or do not want to tell a family member is also important. Rather than saying, "I can't possibly tell Grandpa," try to discover why you feel you cannot. Of course, you *can*—are physically able to— tell Grandpa. What you mean is, "I *choose* not to tell him." You may have excellent reasons for not sharing your information with him, and it will help you if you understand what these reasons are.

Too often we give away our power over circumstances unnecessarily, because we fail to understand the destructive impact of imprecise thinking. When you say, "I *can't* tell Grandpa," you are encouraging yourself to think of him as strong and of yourself as helpless. You may *choose* not to tell him because he has demonstrated a closed mind on the subject of homosexuality and you do not care to mount an assault on his prejudices at this time. You may need your energy for activities that are likely to be more productive. Or you may feel the information would close a door between you and a relative who may die within a few years, and you want to keep this door open. Be realistic about what you can deal with and what you do not care to deal with at this time, realistic about the reasons for your decision.

The difference between feeling you cannot tell and choosing not to tell may seem like a minor point to you, a game with words. Yet your phrasing can have an impact on whether you view yourself as a victim without control of the situation or as a responsible person who has control and can therefore look at the options and make a decision. All of us at various times in our lives are victims of happenings we have not chosen, that have been imposed on us by circumstances beyond our control. What we *do* control are our responses to the circumstances. When you confront a situation realistically you can decide whether you are willing to pay the price of the action you propose to take. If Grandpa is very old and has a serious heart disorder, you may choose to say nothing of your child's sexual orientation. You have weighed the factors involved and have made a choice.

If you believe that telling a close friend about your child's lesbianism or gayness would be the end of the friendship, you need to assess, realistically, this person's value to you. Why is he or she important to you? What do you get from the relationship that you do not want to sacrifice at this time? Whenever you feel helpless in the hands of another person you need to examine the hidden dynamics of the relationship if you are to remain healthy emotionally. Unconsciously, you may be giving the person power over your life that it is not necessary or desirable for you to give.

Conversely, you need to be aware of the realities of your situation. Is your job at stake? Is your friendship with a particular person very meaningful to you? Why? Is your position in a group—whether in church, in an organization, or in the community—at stake? Any of these situations is possible, and genuine wisdom would counsel you to keep your mouth shut in such a case.

Undeniably, there *are* obstacles to coming out, both for parents and for the lesbian or gay person. Society may exact a heavy penalty through job loss (or at least lack of advancement), through social rejection and ostracism, and through other forms of discrimination. Count the cost *before* taking action, rather than after. If you are not anxious to be a hero or heroine at this particular time in your life, you can *choose* not to be.

Also recognize that no one should try to choose the heroic role for another. I think especially of two different sets of parents of two gay men. Both sets of parents live in small towns and belong to theologically conservative churches. The father of each of these men is in a business that could be severely affected by community attitudes toward him. There are younger children in each case whom the fathers want to see through college, and each man is heading toward retirement in ten or fifteen years.

Should these men come out before their small communities as the fathers of gay sons and possibly jeopardize their businesses, their ability to provide for their younger children's education, their and their wives' social and religious life in the community, and their security in retirement? In cases like these, both parents and their same-sex-oriented children need to consider carefully all aspects of the situation. The heroic gesture is easier to make when one is younger and can more easily get another job or when one has no dependents. It is considerably more difficult to assume a heroic role when one has spent a lifetime in a particular community and has a standing it is important to maintain in order to cope with life. If you, parent or same-sex-oriented child, are going to be open about yourself, count the realistic cost beforehand, and be willing to pay whatever price may be exacted of you. If you decide not to make any disclosure at this time in your life, you need not condemn yourself or accept condemnation from another. Obviously, there are realistic reasons for remaining semicloseted, or else writing and reading books like this would not be necessary. You are treading a circular path: It is difficult to come out because of society's present attitudes, and yet society's attitudes are not likely to change until more people come out.

Both you and your lesbian or gay child should keep in mind that, although you may not be ready to come out now in a particular situation, this does not necessarily mean you will never be ready. Perhaps a year or two from now you will be able to do what seems impossible today. And if you are never ready, this is your privilege as a self-directing person. For your child to try to force you to do something is no more acceptable than for you to try to force your adult child into a particular course of action.

A different situation may arise if your child is an activist and appears in the media, making statements concerning gay and lesbian issues or marching in Gay Pride Week parades or taking part in picketing or sit-ins. In this case you may not have much choice as to whether or not you are going to come out of your parents-of-a-homosexual closet. Under these circumstances, if you are having a great deal of trouble dealing with your forced expulsion from the parental closet, you may want to consider seeking help from a trained counselor. It is surprising what good things can result sometimes from situations that initially appear dire or threatening. If you have been kicked from your comfortable berth, make every effort to come to terms with your particular problem, and retrieve all you can from what may seem, at first, to be a disastrous situation.

Seeking professional help is not easy. Perhaps one of the most difficult and courageous acts a person can perform is to pick up the phone and make an appointment for counseling. There is something within everybody that stubbornly resists such a step. Making an effort to reach out for help, however, is a positive choice that indicates strength rather than weakness. Sometimes the only means of moving away from the dead center of indecision is to say, "Right or wrong, I'm going to do this. If it turns out wrong, I'll try something else." Do whatever is necessary for you to come to terms with your circumstances.

What if you or your child is not ready to come out to aunts, uncles, cousins, grandparents, and so on, and yet these people periodically needle you and your child with questions about when Joe or Joanne is going to start dating or get married?

One of the best ways of dealing with such questions comes from a lesbian whose mother spoke of it on a nationwide television program. The young woman's grandmother had been asking her when she was going to get married. Her reply to her grandmother's question went something like this: "If I could be happy without being married, would you be happy for me?"

The basic approach of this answer can be adapted to many different situations. Two things are implicitly stated: The answerer perceives caring on the part of the questioner and appreciates it, but what makes one person happy does not always do the same for another.

If you and your child decide to come out to other family members, remember that these family members may experience some grief reactions. They, too, are having a piece of disquieting information given to them that asks them to rearrange their perceptions and confront a sexual orientation with which they may be uncomfortable. Remember also that their initial reaction will not necessarily be the same as the feeling they may have later.

What about gatherings of the extended family at holidays and other occasions? Because such gatherings can present problems for the family with a lesbian or gay member who has a lover but is not yet "out" to the wider relationship, the Families of Gays and Lesbians group to

which I belonged once planned a meeting around the topic "Can holiday family gatherings be happy—and gay?"
The group zeroed in on the subject from four angles:

1. If the gay or lesbian person has a lover, can he or she join the family group?
2. How does one explain the lover's presence to Grandma, Grandpa, Aunt Elizabeth, Uncle Harold—or even to younger siblings and cousins?
3. Do you (as parents) even *want* your child's lover to join the celebration?
4. How might your lesbian or gay child feel if you do not want the significant other at the festivities?

Although you may not have been aware of it before, suddenly you realize that these traditional family get-togethers are governed by unwritten but rather inflexible guidelines that do not include those unrelated by blood or marriage. You may feel that including a "friend of Joe's (Joanne's)" is the same as announcing your child's sexual orientation. (Possibly you are supersensitive about this and others might not draw this conclusion.)

The patterns that are "always" followed at such get-togethers can impart a sense of compulsion. Carl Whitaker remarks in *The Family Crucible*, that it is difficult to be unfaithful to the rules of one's family, even though these rules may be largely unspoken.[1] What you "always do" on such occasions carries with it its own enforcement, and you may find it exceedingly difficult to break out of established patterns. Obviously, a different course of action will have to be taken, difficult as it may seem to you.

Your problem may be that the extended family is unaware of your child's sexual orientation—or it may be that the family is only too aware and does not want her or him at the gathering, much less her or his lover.

Whatever course of action your immediate family takes

should be a joint decision, and as I have noted repeatedly, joint decisions are not arrived at easily, because they involve honesty about each person's real feelings. To say, "It doesn't matter to me," when it does matter, or "That's fine with me," when it really is not, only lays the groundwork for more difficulties in the future.

Whatever your family's situation there *is* a solution: It begins with honesty to yourself about your wishes and desires and a real listening to the honest feelings of other family members. Silent martyrdom has no place in a situation like this, nor does an uncritical feeling that you are in a trap from which you cannot extricate yourself.

Whenever you feel you have to conform to the pattern of previous years it is time to investigate why you feel this way. What are the unconscious pressures you are experiencing? Try to dig them out. What alternative arrangements can be made? If you follow a certain course of action one year, you do not necessarily have to follow it another year. You can decide (as a family) that "this year we will do what Mother and Dad want," and next year you will celebrate in the way the children want. You can decide that this is the year to take a short trip over Christmas. Maybe this decision *is* running away from the problem. What is wrong with that if it gets you through the holiday season? By the time next Christmas rolls around you may not need to run.

Perhaps the time has come to make a bold decision. One mother I know, who is a widow, has chosen to celebrate holidays with her son and his lover, neither of whom is welcome at the holiday gatherings of her other children and their families. Her straight children are not happy with her decision and have suggested that it would be fairer to celebrate some holidays with them and some with her gay son. She is a woman who knows her own priorities. She has told her straight children that they have their spouses, their siblings, and their children at holidays, and that until they include their brother and his mate, she will celebrate holidays with these two. Despite this one point of contention she maintains a good relationship with her other children and their spouses and sees them and her grandchildren at other times.

It *is* possible to break with traditional patterns, but often it is not easy to do so. Much depends on where you, as parents, are in terms of dealing with your child's sexual orientation. What you find impossible to do this year may be possible in a year or two. Situations that are very difficult now may one day be not nearly so difficult.

Coming out for your child has probably been a long, slow, step-by-step process. It is not likely to be much different for parents.

Chapter 9

Religious Issues and a Same-sex Orientation

When I found out that Eric is gay my difficulty in dealing with his orientation centered in my religious beliefs. Although many (if not most) parents have trouble accepting their child's lesbianism or gayness, religion is not often an issue. In some cases, however, as in mine, religion is—or seems to be—the primary issue.

This chapter deals, to a small extent, with some Jewish viewpoints and, in a more extended fashion (because I am more familiar with this), with an evangelical-fundamental-charismatic theological position, which, for the sake of brevity, is generally referred to in the chapter as a conservative viewpoint.

For easier reference the chapter is divided in four sections: Some Jewish Viewpoints; What Does the Bible Say About Homosexuality?; What Some Conservative Writers Say About Homosexuality; and "Is My Child Lost for Eternity?"

Several books and articles listed in the section "For Further Reading" can provide more information on Jewish viewpoints.

At the end of this book are also listed several books written from a Christian viewpoint that throw a different light on the biblical passages generally believed to deal with homosexuality. Although these interpretations differ from the usual conservative stance, it is helpful for Christians to understand that there are various interpretations, made by earnest, dedicated Christian scholars.

For both Jewish and Christian parents, I call attention to the wisdom of Gamaliel, which he set forth in a situation totally unrelated to homosexuality. Nevertheless, the principle is valid in dealing with religious issues: "If this plan or this undertaking is of men, it will fail; but if it is of God, you will not be able to overthrow them. You might even be found opposing God! [Acts 5:38-39]."

Some Jewish Viewpoints

Many Jewish parents, depending on the way they interpret the Jewish scriptures, feel great anguish about a child's same-sex orientation because of their religion. Some of these parents deal with their pain over this issue by saying Kaddish (the prayer for the dead) for a lesbian or gay child. From this point on these parents consider their child dead. Are other Jewish responses possible? If so, what might they be?

In order to find out I contacted a number of Jewish persons and groups concerning the subject of a same-sex orientation and received diverse responses.

My question about their position on homosexuality to the Lubavitch—a group of the Hasidim, who themselves are a group within the Orthodox Jewish tradition—brought the quick, firm reply, "Homosexuality is taboo."

In 1977 the General Assembly of the Union of American Hebrew Congregations, representing the Reform Movement in North America, adopted the following resolution regarding the human rights of same-sex-oriented persons:

HUMAN RIGHTS OF HOMOSEXUALS

A statement adopted by the General Assembly of the Union of American Hebrew Congregations November 18–22, 1977—San Francisco, California

WHEREAS the UAHC has consistently supported civil rights and civil liberties for all persons, and

WHEREAS the Constitution guarantees civil rights to all individuals,

BE IT THEREFORE RESOLVED that homosexual persons are entitled to equal protection under the law. We oppose discrimination against homosexuals in areas of opportunity, including employment and housing. We call upon our society to see that such protection is provided in actuality.

BE IT FURTHER RESOLVED that we affirm our belief that private sexual acts between consenting adults are not the proper province of government and law enforcement agencies.

BE IT FURTHER RESOLVED that we urge congregations to conduct appropriate educational programming for youth and adults so as to provide greater understanding of the relation of Jewish values to the range of human sexuality.

Jewish Family and Children's Service of Minneapolis, which ministers to those from the whole theological spectrum of the Jewish faith, assured me that in no way did they discriminate against same-sex-oriented persons or their families. "We minister to need," they said. "We do not judge."

When I asked a Jewish lesbian who is in a position to understand the religious community in some depth about the Jewish position regarding homosexuality, she replied along these lines (this is not a word-for-word transcription of our conversation):

There is no one position that all Orthodox, Conservative, or Reform Jews take concerning homosexuality. Even within the three traditions there is no unanimity. It depends on who is doing the interpreting of the scriptures. If you find that your rabbi or the people in your synagogue are rigidly anti-homosexual, find yourself another group of Jewish people who will accept you. There are some. As far as parents are concerned, many use their professed religiosity to maintain their anti-homosexual beliefs. In other words, they use their religious beliefs to rationalize a cultural prejudice.

A long talk with Rabbi Moshe Adler, of the B'nai B'rith Hillel Foundation at the University of Minnesota, brought forth a number of ideas to provide food for thought. He pointed out that rabbis perform two functions, which he called the magisterial function and the pastoral function. The magisterial function refers to the authoritative teaching of Jewish law and ethics, seeking to define what is right and what is wrong. The pastoral function refers to caring for the needy and the hurt, regardless of their level of religious belief or practice. Rabbi Adler said:

When same-sex-oriented persons or their families come to a rabbi, the rabbi should deal with them primarily in a pastoral way, acting out through his own compassion the love of God. Gay or lesbian people and their families come to the rabbi because they want to know that God still loves them and that their own religious community will not cast them out.

You know, God gives us laws as disciplines to holiness, not as mere exercises in obedience. Because God is both just and compassionate God's laws must be construed to reflect that balance of justice with compassion. For this reason, I believe, God's law does not demand heterosexuality of a person for whom this is an impossibility. It seems to me that, in this matter as in all others, the Torah's directive presupposes a person's ability to make a moral choice in full freedom and not under duress. Someone who can choose to "swing" either way, sexually speaking, can meaningfully be commanded to limit his or her "swinging" to one way and not another. It is within the justice of God that he command us and expect our freely given compliance. Here, as in the dietary laws, for example, the commandments discipline our appetites by requiring that we satisfy them in a manner sanctioned by the Creator. Where, however, homosexuality is not simply a matter of satisfying one's appetites, but is the only manner in which a person is able to give and receive adult love and thereby make a loving commitment to another human being, it cannot, I would argue, come under the Torah's prohibition.

Rabbi Adler went on to point out that the community is often selective about the sins for which it excludes people.

Many people violate the Sabbath, but nobody is thrown out of the synagogue or kept from positions of community leadership because of it, even though Sabbath observance is, by both scripture and tradition, the central covenantal institution of Judaism. There's got to be some emotion other than religious zeal behind this anti-homosexual bias.

When the parents of a homosexual person come to me I encourage them to talk at length about their concerns, and then I say, "Before we start looking at any scriptural or Talmudic passages, can you talk about what's really bothering you? What prevents you from accepting your child?" Usually, they're not really talking about religion. The reason they are finding it so difficult to deal with their child's homosexuality is that they themselves have hang-ups about sexuality and sex roles.

Conventional ideas about the roles of men and women make it very hard for a Jewish family to accept a gay or lesbian child. The family, traditionally regarded as the nuclear unit of Jewish life, still tends to assign conventionally sex-based roles to its members. The man is expected to be a tower of strength. The woman is expected to enable the man to come across as this impossible tower of strength, to pick up the pieces when he comes apart under the strain, and to keep herself together lest the family unit collapse. In such a structure a gay son will be seen as effeminate and therefore powerless—not a real man; a lesbian daughter will be seen as masculine and therefore dominating—not a real woman. In either case, parents and children are apt to feel they have failed each other. Mother and father ask, "Where did we go wrong?" Gay son or lesbian daughter asks, "Even though you don't approve of my life-style, can you not love me?"

One of the best things the family can do is go into family therapy and work the whole thing through *together*. The family rabbi can make the referral and continue supplementing the therapy in his pastoral and supportive role.

And what of the Torah? People so often seem to forget that, in addition to prohibiting things, the Pentateuch also commands, "You shall love your neighbor as yourself." Jesus didn't make that up; he was quoting from the Torah. There is a story of a man who came to a Hasidic master and said, "My son is straying. What shall I do with him?" The master replied, "Love him more." This is essentially what I tell parents whose child has just come out to them: Love your gay son or lesbian daughter more, because with all the problems society will put in your child's path, he or she will need your love more urgently than ever.

What Does the Bible Say About Homosexuality?

When I learned about Eric's sexual orientation all my ideas about why homosexuality is unacceptable focused on what I believed the Bible had to say on the subject. I believed in the inerrancy of the Bible, that it is without error in all that it affirms and is the only infallible rule of faith and practice.

How can one argue with a statement like this? It sounds so simple, so irrefutable, so right. If one is going to believe the Bible, one has to believe *all* of it. One cannot pick and choose what one is going to believe or one empties the Word of God of all meaning.

The Bible, however, is not a simple, self-evident book. Let us look at several of the problems encountered in understanding the Bible.

1. *Most of us read from translations of the Bible, rather than from the original Hebrew or Greek manuscripts. For this reason one translation of a passage may state one thing whereas another translation states something different.* This may happen because the translators have worked from more ancient and therefore, presumably, more accurate manuscripts. This also happens because translators are not automatons, and inevitably, they incorporate their own theology and ethics

into their translations. Their choice of the English words they use grows out of their particular theological and ethical position and can represent a particular viewpoint.

John Boswell has put his finger on another difficulty we need to be aware of as we read the Bible.[1] He says that the passage of thousands of years often obscures, sometimes beyond recovery, the exact meaning of words in the languages of ancient people whose experiences and life-styles were very different from ours.

In addition, the original manuscripts physically present many problems. Parts of them may be disintegrating, with the result that words crucial to the meaning of a passage may not be there, gone forever. Hebrew texts were originally written without vowel marks, which were only later introduced to minimize ambiguity. Thus even the most conscientious scholars often have difficulty in making a translation that accurately reflects what the original writer was saying.

While some conservative scholars and many conservative Christians believe God has given us an inerrant original text, God certainly has not given us inerrant translations. In fact, the process of providing us with a Bible would appear, humanly speaking, to be hit and miss. From our finite point of view there would seem to be less possibility of errors creeping in if God had given the biblical message engraved on tablets of stone or cast on gold plates to ensure its survival in one form and one form only.

Yet we find God risking the use of perishable skins, cryptic writing, necessity of translation hundreds or thousands of years after the writing—and not even a sure and certain designation of which manuscripts were the inspired Word of God and which were not.

None of this is intended to indicate that the Bible is *not*

God's word to us. This does mean that often the meaning of a particular passage is difficult to nail down. Why, we might wonder, was the Creator so casual in the methods used to provide us with the Bible?

Divine Truth Versus a Literal Interpretation

2. *Those who say the Bible is the infallible word of God cannot mean that every word of the Bible is historically accurate,* as many conservative biblical scholars believe. Francis Schaeffer spells out the dilemma: "What sense does it make," he asks, "for God to give us true religious truths and at the same time place them in a book that is wrong when it touches history and the cosmos?"[2]

With minimal research one realizes that this *is* what God has done. In Genesis 1 and 2 two different accounts of creation are given and they do not agree. Which account is correct? And although each of the four Gospels tells the story of Christ's life, they differ in many significant ways. For example, in the first three Gospels the Last Supper takes place at the Passover meal. In John's Gospel Jesus is crucified on the day the lambs are sacrificed in the temple for the Passover meal. So in the fourth Gospel the Last Supper takes place before the Passover day. Which account is correct?

John Marsh, in discussing the difference in historical facts among the four Gospels, makes the point that these manuscripts were not written as historical records, but as theological treatises, to highlight particular aspects of God's message through Jesus Christ to humanity.[3]

In commenting on such differences in the Bible, C.S. Lewis has written: "The very *kind* of truth we are often demanding was, in my opinion, never even envisaged by the ancients."[4]

Those who say, "Every word in the Bible must be true historically and scientifically as well as spiritually" are afraid that if people can say parts of the Bible are not accurate in these ways, they can then go on to say, "Why should I believe that Jesus Christ rose from the dead? You can't prove it."

It appears to me that this is why God has gone about giving us the Bible in such a seemingly casual way and has allowed material to be included that is not necessarily historically accurate in every instance. (There are undoubtedly many other reasons. I make no claim to having any direct revelations from God on this subject. I speak as a human being making human deductions from study, observation, and experience.)

"Now faith is the assurance of things hoped for, the conviction of things not seen [Heb. 11:1]." I do not believe God intends to prove the reality of the divine Selfhood in the ways we humans would go about proving it. I therefore believe that the Bible presents to us *divine truths*, which is not the same as saying that every word of the Bible is scientific and historical fact. Moreover, we often have to dig to understand what these truths are; many are not self-evident.

Nor does the Bible contain the answer, in easy prooftext form, to every problem that may arise in anyone's life. Let us look at one well-known example.

For many years the Bible was used to prove that slavery is an acceptable way of treating human beings. Now Christians are using the Bible to show that slavery is incompatible with the Christian view of life. Christians have had to study the message of the Bible as a whole and make deductions from a variety of biblical principles in order to arrive at this conclusion. Not even such a dominant and authoritative figure as Paul made any definite statement against slavery. Instead, he sent a runaway slave back to his master, accompanied by a letter that is now known as the Epistle to Philemon.

Interpreting the Bible's Meaning

3. *If the interior meaning of the Bible is so difficult to discern, and if we have to work so hard, how can we be sure* what *God intended?* Such indefiniteness does not seem fair to us human beings who are trying, with finite minds, to understand and obey an infinite God. It may even threaten us. If we cannot be precisely sure of what God is saying, how can we know we are doing what God wants us to do? How can we *know* we are saved?

I offer a few thoughts in relation to the above questions. First, it appears God preferred to give us a book that would offer enough material to keep the wisest person occupied for a lifetime without ever coming to the end of what the Bible has to offer. In the Bible, God has provided an inexhaustible supply of treasures. These are presented in a form that requires us to read, study, wrestle, think, and pray and that necessitates interaction between God and ourselves in order to understand what any particular passage of the Bible is saying.

Furthermore, there are different levels of meaning. One verse or passage may speak to us truly but superficially at one point in our lives, and at another time we may find this same verse or passage speaking to us more deeply. "Why didn't I ever see it in this light before?" we wonder, because now the truth of which we are suddenly aware seems almost self-evident. The deeper insight comes, of course, because *we* are ready to perceive it, not because the message has changed or because God was not ready to impart it to us before.

Then there is the problem of whether we should interpret the Bible in light of the conditions that prevailed at the time each particular book was written or whether we should accept the precepts contained in the Bible as a message given once but applicable as it stands to all eras.

It is difficult to make a good case for the latter position without getting into many problems. We cannot take every statement in the Bible at face value and try to put it into practice or, among other things, we would be putting people to death for adultery (Leviticus 20:10); no person born out of wedlock—or for that matter that person's descendants for ten generations—would be allowed in church (Deuteronomy 23:2); and the roof of every house would have to have a railing around it (Deuteronomy 22:8).

4. *We cannot understand what the Bible is saying to us today* until *we understand what the conditions were at the time those words were written, and therefore what those words really mean. Only then can we understand what* underlying truths or principles *we should apply to our present-day situations.* Otherwise, we arrive at erroneous conclusions as to what we should or should not be doing. Even those who believe in the "literal" interpretation of the Bible have to rationalize their nonadherence to many of the Bible's directives.

It is enlightening that present-day careful research into Paul's writings reveals Paul in a new light with respect to the position of women. If we read 1 Corinthians 14: 34-35, for example, against the background of conditions in Paul's day, we discover that the Greek word translated as speak is *lalein,* which "refers primarily to utterance rather than meaningful communication," according to Richard and Catherine Clark Kroeger.[5] The writer of an ancient dictionary defined the term as "to talk nonsense." Knowing that in certain pagan Greek rituals "frenzied shouting was expected from women and considered a necessary ingredient" of worship, one begins to realize that Paul *was* speaking to specific difficulties that occurred, because his congregation was made up of newly converted pagans.

In further clarification of the passage the Kroegers say

that "women were encouraged to question their husbands at home, since the women had usually been denied an opportunity for education." "For it is shameful for a woman to speak in church," Paul wrote, in 1 Corinthians 14:35. If he was referring to gossip or meaningless pagan shouting, this throws a new light on the real meaning of the passage.

What Does the Bible Really Say About Homosexuality?

Some theologians and scholars feel that, at times, Paul was in error in what he said, that his wisdom was not infallible. Certainly we know that in some instances Paul makes a distinction between his human instructions to a congregation and specific ones he has received from God (1 Corinthians 7: 10, 12, 25; 2 Corinthians 11:17).

But if we might have *misinterpreted* Paul's teachings about women, might we also have misinterpreted the biblical passages dealing with homosexual acts? Notice that I did not say *homosexuality*. The Bible does not deal with homosexuality in the sense of giving guidance for those who have a same-sex orientation to life. The Bible speaks only of certain same-sex abuses: attempted gang rape (Genesis 19 and Judges 19), lust as an expression of idolatry (Romans 1), and what seems to be exploitative and extortionistic homosexual prostitution (Leviticus 18:22; 20:13; 1 Corinthians 6:9; 1 Timothy 1:10). The Bible says nothing, as Virginia Mollenkott points out, about a *same-sex orientation* or about homosexual *love*.[6]

Reread the story of Sodom and Gomorrah and you will notice the following points:

- The men of Sodom wanted to *gang-rape* the two visitors to the city. (Homosexual gang-rape was a standard practice in those days by which conquering armies humiliated their fallen foes.)
- One would not suppose the whole population of

Sodom was homosexual, or why would Lot have moved there in the first place, why would two of the men be betrothed to Lot's daughters, and why would Lot have offered the men his daughters to distract them from demanding his guests?

- What the men of Sodom were proposing was the *gang-rape of God's messengers*. This introduces the dimension of attempting to degrade the Hebrew God.

The real sins of Sodom, according to Ezekiel 16: 49-50, seem to have been "pride, surfeit of food, and prosperous ease"; not aiding the poor and needy; and being "haughty" and doing "abominable things" before God. Strong's *Exhaustive Concordance of the Bible* gives "idolatrous actions" as one of the meanings of the Hebrew word translated as "abominable things."[7]

In the New Testament Jesus refers to Sodom and Gomorrah in connection with the rejection of his message in various cities (Matthew 10:15; 11:23-24; Luke 10:12). There is no connection between Sodom's sexual behavior and Jesus' condemnation of these cities. Rather, he appears to be referring to Sodom's violation of the almost sacred ancient Eastern code of caring for the wayfarer within a city's gates.

In Leviticus 18:22 and 20:13 there is no doubt that the writer is condemning homosexual acts. Or is there? John Boswell points out that the Hebrew word translated as abomination "does not usually signify something intrinsically evil, like rape or theft," but rather something that is ritually unclean for Jews, like eating pork or engaging in intercourse during menstruation.[8]

That the act described in Leviticus 18:22 could be connected with the worship of idols is also indicated by the fact that the previous verse prohibits the sacrifice of one's children (*Revised Standard Version* translation) to Molech. In the *King James Version* "children" is translated as "seed," leading Boswell to comment that "the prohibition of homosexual acts follows immediately upon a prohibition of idolatrous sexuality. . . . 'And thou shalt not let any of thy seed pass through the fire to Molech.' "[9]

Again, Strong's *Concordance* provides us with a different understanding of "abomination," giving "idolatry" or "an idol" as meanings. In fact, it says, "especially idolatry."[10] If we read verse 22 with this translation—"You shall not lie with a man as with a woman: it is idolatry"—we get a different understanding of the verse, especially taken in conjunction with verse 21.

The translators of the *Revised Standard Version* reinforce the idea of pagan prostitution by citing Deuteronomy 23:18 as a reference for Leviticus 18:22. God forbids the bringing of "the hire of a harlot, or the wages of a dog"— footnoted as a sodomite or male prostitute—"into the house of the Lord your God in payment for any vow." It becomes clearer, as we understand what the original Hebrew words meant, that the law prohibited *idolatrous* homosexual *acts,* not a homosexual orientation to life.

In Romans 1:18-32 the main drive of the passage is that the gentiles (pagans) ought to have recognized God's sovereignty and holiness because they could see it all around them in nature. Instead, they foolishly worshiped idols. Because of this, God gave them up to *lust.* An example of this lust is given in verses 26 and 27, and then Paul reverts to his main argument, that because they did not acknowledge God, the Creator gave them up to a base mind and improper conduct. Interestingly, in the intensive catalog of their sins that Paul lists in verses 29-31, homosexual acts are not mentioned by name. Again in this passage homosexual acts are mentioned only in the context of idolatry, as an example of what happens to idolaters. The passage as a whole focuses not on homosexual acts, but on idolatry.[11]

Idolatry, Paganism, and Homosexual Acts

The obvious connection the Bible makes between idolatry and homosexual acts has not been lost on several conservative writers and scholars. I was interested to discover that they go to some length to prove that a present-day same-sex orientation is wrong because it is idolatrous. For instance, after making connections between homosexual behavior and idolatry, Richard Lovelace writes: "The homosexuality of any given individual is not the direct punishment of his or her idolatry, but is a product of the damaged social fabric in a society of idolaters."[12] He goes on to say that the most serious forms of sin dealt with in the Bible "are not conscious, voluntary acts of disobedience to known laws." Rather, they are unconscious attitudes that manifest themselves in compulsive outward behavior. Because "human sin and God's punishment upon it have deeply affected the processes by which sexual identity is formed," he says, "none of us, heterosexual or homosexual, naturally desires to fulfill perfectly God's plan for our sexuality. We did not consciously choose to have the *deviant sexual orientation which drives us toward fornication, adultery, or homosexual practice.*" We *are* confronted, he says, with the choice of whether or not we should "act out our orientation and fulfill our natural desires."[13]

But are fornication and adultery sexual orientations, like heterosexuality and homosexuality? The responsible answer has to be no. Obviously, Lovelace is not searching for unbiased truth. Instead he is making a case against homosexuality and is willing to compare forms of behavior that are not comparable at all to make his point. He is proving a previously held idea by redefining meanings of words to suit his purpose.

John N. Oswalt makes a more elaborate connection between homosexuality and paganism, of which idolatry is one manifestation. He gives a long, detailed, involved, and carefully developed argument covering sixty pages. The argument revolves around the central idea that "the purpose of pagan religion was to insure that human beings could shape divine and natural events to enhance their own security."[14] Because this undermined the omnipotence of the true God, paganism was evil and therefore homosexuality had to be evil also, since it was connected with pagan practice.

The problem is that Oswalt is trying to understand the symbolic, archetypal thinking and practices found in pagan religion through logical, analytical thinking. This is similar to trying to analyze the impact of a Beethoven symphony by finding out how many times during the work the composer has used each note on the staff. Oswalt is trying to understand a particular phenomenon in a way that cannot lead to understanding it.

In comparing analytical thought with symbolic thought Morton Kelsey says: "One is the thinking of logic and science, the other the thinking of imagination, of poetry, art and religion, and also of dreams."[15] The personalities and characteristics of pagan gods and goddesses were not arrived at through any logical, analytical process. Rather, they were personifications of human desires for power, freedom, happiness, and so on, as well as of human foibles. Because these personifications arose spontaneously as unconscious projections rather than as conscious creations (no one decided to make up these personifications; they "grew" and developed in people's imaginations over long periods), they had about them a mystical or supernatural aura. They were perceived as gods and goddesses by those who were their creators.

The worship of these deities was grounded in the limited, unscientific understanding of a world unacquainted with the kind of science we know and understand. The fertility of the fields could be increased, they believed, through fertility rituals involving people. They worshiped the sun in order to keep it alive to provide light and warmth for the earth. They danced before the gods who governed the rain so drought would not occur. They did not—could not—understand that fertility in the fields results, not from ritual human sexual intercourse, but from the right combination of minerals, warmth, light, and moisture; that sacrifices of human life will not keep the sun alive; and that dancing will not bring rain.

Oswalt builds his whole case against homosexuality on the idea that homosexual activity is a manifestation of a pagan world view that recognizes no boundaries, no limits, no areas as being out of bounds.[16] The Bible imposes certain limitations, he says, because "behavior without limits serves and models a world view that is directly antithetical to the truth."[17] One need not keep an image or be a cult prostitute, he says, to be living a life that denies the transcendence of God, as he says the pagans did. "One needs only to live as though he were the sole arbiter of right and wrong in his life, as though there were nothing to prevent him from doing what he wanted. Those who do so are living according to the pagan world view."[18]

In summing up Oswalt says the Bible prohibits all persons from engaging in homosexual activity, even if they have a same-sex orientation to life, because such activity is "a falsification of the created order of God. To condone it is to condone an entire world view that is at variance with the truth."[19] This is a large conclusion to draw from a few verses scattered throughout the Bible, particularly since Jesus never specifically addressed the subject.

Even a modest acquaintance with pagan religions leads to the realization that, rather than having been developed as a diabolical means of leading people astray, they are instead imperfect and limited perceptions of God's created order. They attempt to explain the puzzling events that took place in the world. Pagan religions were filled with gods and goddesses who were, in large measure, unconscious projections of their creators' own humanness but who also reflected, in flawed form, eternal truths imperfectly perceived. How else can one account for the Dying and Rising God, who appeared in many pagan religions and who foreshadowed Christ—the perfect consummation of these dimly perceived hopes and dreams?

Of course the pagans tried to control their world. If we did not understand scientific cause and effect, which enables us to control our world at least to a degree, no doubt we also would attempt to ensure our security through superstitious beliefs and practices. Whether we realize it or not, our faith is evolving, and many of the beliefs of medieval Christians, for example, now appear to us as hardly more than slightly sanctified superstition. In all likelihood our twentieth-century Christian faith will appear primitive to Christians a thousand years from now, should the world endure that long.

To argue that we cannot condone homosexual activity today because it represents a philosophical concept hostile to the sovereignty of God seems, to me, to be an elaborate case of overkill that also misses the target. I believe Oswalt's thesis results from a misreading of history, a misunderstanding of biblical texts, and an ignorance of the springs of human personality and action. It also seems to be an indication that the earlier defenses of conservative religious thinking against homosexuality have been effectively demolished, and that it is now necessary to go farther afield in order to prove that God cannot, under any circumstances, condone a same-sex orientation or genital sexual activity between persons of the same sex.

Two more biblical passages deal with homosexuality: 1 Corinthians 6:9-10 and 1 Timothy 1:10. Or do they? John Boswell points out that one of the two Greek words in 1 Corinthians 6:9—which in a number of translations has been coupled with the other Greek word and translated as homosexual—means, basically, soft. It is used in Matthew 11:8 with this meaning and elsewhere in the New Testament as "sick" (see Matthew 4:23; 9:35; and 10:1).

"In a specifically moral context," Boswell writes, "it very frequently means 'licentious,' 'loose,' or 'wanting in self-control.'" He goes on to point out that "the word is never used in Greek to designate gay people as a group" or even to refer to homosexual acts as a type of behavior. Often, he says, it occurs in other writings from the same period as Paul's letters in reference to heterosexual persons or activity.[20]

The second Greek word, which appears in 1 Corinthians 6:9 and in 1 Timothy 1:10, seems to be used, according to Boswell, more in connection with male prostitute than to denote homosexuality.

Few of us are knowledgable enough to know what the Hebrew or Greek of the original manuscripts is saying. We have to rely on what the translators think most closely approximates the original meanings, and as we have seen, translators do have biases. In the end we accept a translation on trust—trust in the person or persons who have made the translation. We can do nothing else. And we are likely to trust the translation that most nearly meshes with our already-held beliefs and with our unconscious fears and projections.

A further observation concerning translations deals with the English word sodomite, used in the *King James Version* and several other versions of the Bible. "No Hebrew or Greek word formed on the name 'Sodom' ever appears in the biblical manuscripts on which these versions are based," says Victor Furnish. In every instance in the *King James Version* where the word sodomite is used, "the reference is to male prostitutes associated with places of worship." He further points out that the Old Testament text attacks male prostitutes, not because they had sexual relationships with other males, but rather (as also in the case of female prostitutes) because they were serving alien gods.[21]

As this brief sampling indicates, there are many possible ways of translating and interpreting the biblical passages dealing with homosexual acts. Usually, we tend to read only those authors whose theology coincides with our own and will therefore reinforce our beliefs. We do not believe that the others could be right. They may have done a great deal of research—we may be willing to concede this—but *they do not really know the Lord.* How could they and still write the things they do?

But perhaps we are not allowing the real message of the scriptures to come through. Perhaps we are putting God in the box of our own cultural prejudices and biases. Uncomfortable and threatening as this idea may be, you owe it to yourself and your gay or lesbian child to try to read with an open mind. Such scholars as Furnish, Boswell, the Rev. John McNeill, Letha Scanzoni, and Virginia Mollenkott carefully document the reasons for their interpretations of these passages.[22] It is impossible to make an intelligent appraisal on any subject without looking at both sides of the question.

There is *no perfect interpretation* of the Bible, just as there is no perfect translation. We choose to believe what we feel comfortable with. You can choose to believe the conservative writers who hammer away at the idea that a same-sex relationship is sinful because it is a same-sex relationship. Or you can choose to believe what would seem to be a more accurate understanding of biblical manuscripts. God has given no one person or group a complete and unerring interpretation of the Bible from beginning to end. Had God wanted to give such an interpretation, this could have been accomplished. It would seem, instead, that the divine intention is for human beings to struggle with the biblical material, to learn and grow as they interact with it in the light of new knowledge, both religious and scientific, and thus to move continually onward in humankind's struggle from the Garden of Eden to the New Jerusalem.

What Some Conservative Writers Say About Homosexuality

When I was in the process of coming to grips with Eric's same-sex orientation I wanted to know what conservative religious writers were saying about homosexuality. Although I went to several evangelical bookstores, I could find only *one book*—and the salesperson had great difficulty locating it. Apparently, homosexuality was not a subject conservative writers wanted to deal with, or conservative publishers to publish.

Now all this has changed. You can walk into almost any evangelical bookstore and find a goodly stock of books dealing with homosexuality, most of them anti-same-sex orientation. There has been a publishing explosion. Evidently, the condemnation of homosexuality is an item that sells. You can easily and thoroughly reinforce your ideas that homosexuality is an abomination before God and that homosexual persons "will not inherit the kingdom of God," if you so desire.

Although I have read many of these books, for several reasons the writers fail to persuade me that they unerringly represent God's ideas about a same-sex orientation.

One school of thought, the more rigid and absolute, says that a person must become completely heterosexual in order to be acceptable to God. The other school of thought is content to accept the fact that many same-sex-oriented persons cannot change their orientation, and God, it says, does not condemn the orientation—*so long as the person lives a celibate life*. The homosexual *acts* are wrong, not the orientation.

Right away I am faced with a dilemma. Which school of thought *really* represents what God intends? How can I know which is right? I am back where I started: I must choose which idea of God's truth I am going to accept.

Personally, I find great difficulty subscribing to either view. I cannot go along with the first, because I have read the writings of enough respected scientific researchers to believe that, in most cases, it is impossible to change one's sexual orientation. I cannot believe that God rejects a person because of a condition the person did not choose and cannot change.

Celibacy and Salvation

I also find difficulty with the second view, that in order to be acceptable to God a person must refrain from any genital expression within a committed same-sex relationship. When we say this to a lesbian or a gay man what we are really saying is that to be saved she or he *must* remain celibate. This sounds unpleasantly like, "By works are you saved," rather than by faith. Paul wrote in the letter to the Ephesians: "For by grace you have been saved through faith; and this is not your own doing, it is the gift of God—not because of works, lest any man should boast [2:8-9]." The framework of belief and salvation could be significantly altered by trying to make celibacy the touchstone of a person's (another person's!) salvation.

On a less theological level, I wonder how long celibacy

would remain an issue for these writers if the situation were reversed. If other-sex-oriented persons knew that their kind of sexual relations would prevent them from going to heaven, that only homosexual relations were approved, I wonder whether they might not decide to let their eternal salvation take care of itself and live as they saw fit now.

Celibacy is not something we dare *impose* on someone else. It can only be freely chosen by the person who will have to live out the choice. Donald Goergen, a Dominican who has studied at the Kansas Neurological Institute and the Menninger Foundation, has had the task of counseling with those who are in the process of deciding whether or not to commit themselves to a celibate life. The questions he asks them to consider carefully throw a new light on the matter of celibacy.

Here are some of the questions:

What is it about celibacy that you find attractive? Why would you choose to be celibate? What does celibacy mean to you? What does the notion of "call" mean to you? What are the practical problems raised by a celibate life-style? Are you willing to undertake these? . . . Are you personally capable of the commitment celibacy requires? . . . How do you want to use your celibacy? How can you increasingly integrate it into the person you are coming to be?[23]

There is a stronger and more positive reason for embracing the legitimacy of same-sex genital expression. James B. Nelson has expressed this position in his book *Embodiment*, summarizing the position taken by theologian Norman Pittenger: "God's abiding purpose for humankind is that in response to divine action we should realize our intended humanity as human lovers—in the richest, broadest, and most responsible sense of the term. Our embodied sexuality is the physiological and psychological base for our capacity to love."

Abnormality or deviance, Pittenger feels, should not be measured statistically, but rather against the

norm of humanity in Jesus Christ. Gay persons desire and need deep and lasting relationships just as do heterosexuals, and appropriate genital expression should be denied to neither.

Thus, the ethical question which Pittenger poses is this: what sexual behavior will serve and enhance, rather than inhibit, damage, or destroy the fuller realization of our divinely-intended humanity? The answer is sexual behavior in accord with an ethics of love. This means commitment and trust, tenderness, respect for the other, and the desire for ongoing and responsible communion with the other. On the negative side, an ethics of love mandates against selfish sexual expression, cruelty, impersonal sex, obsession with sex, and against actions done without willingness to take responsibility for the consequences. Such an ethics always asks about the meanings of acts in their total context—in the relationship itself, in society, and in regard to God's intended direction for human life. Such an ethics of sexual love is equally appropriate to heterosexual and gay Christians. There is no double standard.[24]

Misinformation and Wishful Thinking

Another reason why the books by conservative authors fail to persuade me is that I found a lot of misinformation and wishful thinking in the conservative religious books I read. I have already given examples of this in dealing with the interpretation of several biblical passages. There are many others.

Tim LaHaye, for instance, in his book *The Unhappy Gays,* makes many statements without including any information about how he arrived at these conclusions.

"No one is born homosexual, nor is it something over which he has no control—unless he *thinks* he has no control over his sexual direction," LaHaye says, without giving any evidence to support this conclusion.[25]

John Money, a behavioral endocrinologist at Johns Hopkins University, who has spent years in scientific research into human sexuality, gives some indications of the utter complexity of human sexual development in his book *Sexual Signatures.* He speaks of the continual interaction between heredity and environment in making us the particular, unique person each of us is.[26] He also speaks about critical prenatal influence.[27] He writes of "obligative homosexuals," those who are able to respond erotically *"only* to others of the same sex, in fantasy and usually in fact."[28]

In contrast to Money's conclusions from carefully controlled research, LaHaye does not hesitate to list eight factors that supposedly "predispose" a person to a same-sex orientation.[29] Evidently he has read Irving Bieber's book *Homosexuality,* because LaHaye dwells emphatically on the supposed parental role in causing homosexuality.[30] What he does not realize is that Bieber's statistics were gathered more than twenty years ago from a population who came to his consulting room because they were experiencing difficulties in dealing with life—at a time, we need to realize, when homosexuality was a crime in many states and when society had imposed severer sanctions on it than now.

We also need to remember that in the years when Bieber was collecting his statistics it was automatically assumed that a same-sex-oriented person's unhappiness stemmed from his or her sexual orientation, rather than from society's repressive and hostile attitudes toward same-sex-oriented persons.

In another instance LaHaye was told by an unnamed psychologist friend that "homosexuals . . . will lie, cheat, steal, and do almost anything to keep their secret hidden." LaHaye states that he has "never met an exception."[31] It does not seem to occur to him that in many situations lesbians and gay men must hide their sexual orientation to survive. Of course they have lied, but to say they have also cheated and stolen is defamation of the character of thousands of fine, decent people. Some same-sex-oriented persons have done all these things, just as some hetero-sexual persons have done these things. Neither have done them *because* of their sexual orientation.

LaHaye also writes: "Angry people are not happy peo-ple, and it seems that homosexuality foments a hostile way of life."[32] Apparently, it does not occur to him that gay and lesbian persons may be angry—and justifiably so—at the way in which society devalues their person-hood.

"Anyone considering homosexuality as a life style ought to face the realistic fact that it is extremely conducive to rejection," LaHaye says.[33] His assumption seems to be that a person sits down one day and says, "Shall I be straight or gay? Being gay sounds like more fun." As chap-ter 6 demonstrates, nothing could be farther from what actually happens.

Another weakness of his book is that LaHaye seldom quotes an authority by name.[34] My reaction to this type of reference is that if the person had any standing in the scientific community, LaHaye would have used his or her name.

He also leaps to conclusions about interpretation of sta-tistics. "Anyone can see," he writes, "that homosexuality has increased in direct proportion to the increase in pornography."[35] And again "marriage has declined, and births, of course, have dropped off" since laws against homosexuality were struck down in England in 1957.[36] In neither case does he cite statistical studies that would indicate a real connection between homosexuality and his reading of statistics.

LaHaye ends his book on what seems like a paranoid note: "Some people believe"—again I should like a more definite statement of who these people are—"that an international network of homosexuals has been working its way into governments for years."[37] "Some people" may believe this, but are there real, demonstrable occurrences that point in this direction? LaHaye does not mention them. Instead, by means of an undocumented statement, he insinuates that unnamed perils await us at the hands of a sinister group. Look at the statement logically. Suppose this "international network" is indeed "infiltrating governments." For what purpose? LaHaye gives no indication of what we have to fear from the "international network."

I have dwelt at length on LaHaye's book because he is well known in conservative church circles. In many ways his book is easier to read than some of the other anti-gay/lesbian books, and the unwary reader may not understand the difference between statements backed by statistics and claims that are unsupported by demonstrable facts—especially if the author is "proving" those things that the reader already believes or wants to believe.

Is Homosexuality a Sin?

All anti-gay/lesbian books by conservative religious writers start with the same basic premise—that the Bible says homosexuality is a sin—and therein lies a problem. The authors therefore must establish that this is what the

Bible actually says and must prove either that a homosexual orientation to life is consciously chosen and can therefore be consciously changed or that no matter what the original causes, a homosexual orientation to life can be changed to heterosexual. Failing that, the authors need to prove that celibacy can be made to work, since presumably a sexual relationship not blessed by marriage is unacceptable to God.

Different writers take different approaches in trying to prove their point. According to Greg Bahnsen, new understandings about a same-sex orientation toward life are totally irrelevant. So is the cultural background of the biblical writers and their "alleged scientific ignorance." "God does not—and has not been found to—contradict His clear message in Scripture by information revealed through nature, history, or any realm of creation," he writes.[38] (One wonders how he integrates dinosaurs and the formation of coal, for example, into the biblical story of creation.) If we follow this line of reasoning to its logical conclusion, the Bible is the ultimate historical and scientific textbook. As C.S. Lewis said, "the very *kind* of truth we are demanding was often never even envisaged by the ancients."

I always check an author's bibliography to see what books have been used as reference. Almost everything published before 1970 is likely to have an anti-gay bias, because even more than now, this was the tenor of the times. Bahnsen's bibliography is heavy with such books; sixty-nine percent were published before 1970. I distrust books that ignore new information—notice that I said *information,* not theories.

The same is true of Frank DuMas' book *Gay Is Not Good.*[39] Eighty-five percent of his references date from before 1970. Of the remaining books in his bibliography, none was published after 1974. While this may not seem important to the general reader, it is significant to those who are used to dealing with scientific research. DuMas is basing his book on outdated information.

A Case of Eisegesis?

In my reading I have discovered that some conservative writers try to counter arguments put forth by those who believe the Bible is not as anti-homosexual as was once thought. These latter authors have stated that biblical writers were dealing only with specific homosexual acts, not with a homosexual orientation to life, and they have backed up their statements with supporting and confirming evidence. Since only within the past fifty to one hundred years have we known anything about such a condition as a same-sex orientation, their statements make sense to me. Before that, homosexuality was viewed simply as a perversity.

Not so, says Richard Lovelace. Writing about Romans 1:26-27, he says that, in addition to condemning male and female homosexual acts as sinful, this passage also speaks of the homosexual *orientation*, "the erotic drive behind these acts, as 'dishonorable desires.'"[40] Does it? Or has Lovelace fallen into the trap theologians call eisegesis— reading present-day ideas into the interpretation of a biblical text.

John Oswalt is certain biblical writers knew of homosexuality as an orientation. His reasoning is that Paul, as well as writers of the Old Testament, would have encountered it, among the people of Greece and Ionia in Paul's case and among the sophisticated inhabitants of Canaan in the case of the Old Testament writers.[41] But if *nobody* in those days understood it as an orientation, contacts with Greeks, Ionians, and Canaanites would have made no difference in the biblical writers' understanding of homosexuality.

Victor Furnish says that homosexuality in biblical times was seen as the overflow of heterosexual lust so fierce that intercourse with women could no longer satisfy it. He demonstrates this clearly with two quotations from ancient writers.

One is from Chrysostom, a first-century Roman, who wrote that when a man finds there is no scarcity of women (especially prostitutes) and no resistance to his advances, he will feel contempt for such easy conquests and feel scorn for a woman's love. Such a man "will turn his assault against the male quarters," believing that there "he will find a pleasure difficult and hard to procure."[42]

The other quotation is from Philo Judaeus, a Jewish philosopher of Alexandria and a contemporary of the apostle Paul: "Not only in their mad lust for women did they violate the marriages of their neighbors, but also men mounted males without respect for the sex nature which the active partner shares with the passive."[43]

Unfounded Optimism

Other conservative writers I read say that it is not so difficult to change a homosexual orientation. Kenneth Gangel quotes from an article by Charles Young in which the latter writes: "From my own clinical experience in dealing with homosexuals, I believe there is solid ground for optimism for them."[44] No supporting statistics are given, and there is no indication of follow-up some years later to see if the "ground for optimism" was warranted. Gangel also says that "Klaus Bockmühl cites a fifty percent cure rate of homosexuals in the New York Academy of Medical Science Psychiatric Division"—an unprecedented rate of change.[45] If Bockmühl's statistics are accurate, why is he not instructing others in his methods, and why has his success not been more widely publicized?

Jerry Kirk, a Presbyterian minister, says, rather glibly,

"There is hope for the homosexual because God never commands us to do anything without also offering to us the power and the strength by which to obey."[46] Such an unproven statement can be an extremely powerful guilt-producer for those who have striven sincerely with every means at their disposal to alter their sexual orientation and yet have failed. Kirk also says, "I think the success rate is often greater than gays admit. . . . Several therapists report a very high success rate with homosexuals now if their motivation for change is great."[47] Again, this statement is judgmental and guilt-producing for those who have tried to change and failed.

Another writer, William P. Wilson, says that treatment using a number of different approaches will produce successful change in "a high percentage of persons." Successful therapy, he says, depends on "high levels of motivation, previous successful heterosexual performance, and aggressive masculine behavior."[48] Apparently, he is not aware that there have been pro football players who are gay. And what of those who have never performed heterosexually?

Still another writer, William H. McKain Jr., believes that "if God's prescription for the life of a disciple prohibits homosexual practice, we need to have the faith to believe that one or the other of these options"—conversion to a heterosexual orientation or a celibate life-style—"will be attainable to the homosexual person by means of God's grace."[49]

John Money writes differently. He says that "for those who at puberty feel shocked or guilty" when they discover their same-sex orientation, "it's too late to do much about it. The only hope of changing erotic stimulus-response patterns at or after puberty lies in major, long-term, therapeutic reeducation, and it is not a very strong hope."[50]

Some conservative religious persons feel that what may be impossible scientifically is possible through faith and prayer.

C.S. Lewis, in *The World's Last Night*, says: "Prayer is request. The essence of request, as distinct from compulsion, is that it may or may not be granted." He goes on to comment that, although some passages in the New Testament seem "to promise an invariable granting of our prayers," we have only to look at Christ in the Garden of Gethsemane to realize that this cannot be what those passages really mean. "The holiest of all petitioners prayed three times that a certain cup might pass from Him. It did not. After that the idea that prayer is recommended to us as a sort of infallible gimmick may be dismissed."[51]

Can same-sex-oriented persons change? Conservative religious writers are optimistic that they *can* change. They need to be optimistic. Otherwise their whole interpretation of the biblical passages on homosexuality will fall apart, and they seem to believe that if these interpretations disintegrate, their entire understanding of the Bible will also collapse.

Can Same-sex-oriented Persons Really Change?

The matter of change is more complex than conservative writers care to admit. Who are the "homosexuals" who have been treated? Have they lived as same-sex-oriented persons for some time? Have they had a few homosexual encounters? (Alfred Kinsey found that more than thirty-three percent of the male population had had homosexual encounters.[52]) Have they had homosexual fantasies but never a homosexual encounter? Do they fall near the center on the Kinsey scale, indicating that they are not exclusively homosexual, although they find same-sex encounters provide greater emotional and sexual fulfillment than heterosexual encounters?

And those who claim high rates of cure—what do their

follow-up statistics look like? Is the person still satisfied with his or her new heterosexual orientation five years, ten years, fifteen years after treatment? Before I can accept the statement that the heterosexual orientation is permanent, I need to know the person's track record over a period of time. Then I will believe in the reality of that person's changeover.

To facilitate a conversion in sexual orientation many counselors have recommended—and many lesbian and gay persons independent of counselors have undertaken—marriage as a way of changing a same-sex orientation. This seldom works. Heterosexual marriage cannot and should not be used as a method of "curing" a same-sex orientation.

First, if the person has a true same-sex orientation, marriage cannot change it. Even though complete fidelity may exist within the marriage, I am told by those who have experienced it that there is an area of unfulfillment. The actions within the marriage may be completely heterosexual; yet the inner climate of the same-sex-oriented person has not changed. He or she still longs at times for the fulfillment of a same-sex relationship. One married gay man expressed his feelings clearly when he said that in heterosexual intercourse he does not experience the letting down of ego boundaries, the sense of spiritual oneness with the partner that he does in intercourse with another man.

Another reason why marriage should not be used as an attempted cure for a same-sex orientation lies in the word used. An article published in *Christianity Today* tells of Fred, a young homosexual man who wanted to change. Despite some serious doubts he decided to marry. He was open with his fiancée about his sexual orientation and a year after the marriage says he has found her to be his biggest help.

"I need my wife to know when I'm starting to fall away,

and when she sees my eyes cruising some people, she needs to tactfully pull me back in. I need to know that she knows my problem and will not reject me when she finds I'm slipping but pull me back in with love."[53]

At least the wife knew beforehand what she was letting herself in for. But do we "use" a spouse to try to "cure" a same-sex orientation? Fred is asking his wife to be a trainer, a disciplinarian. What happens if Fred's wife tires of her role? What if Fred stops welcoming her help and begins to think of her as nagging? There are enough areas of friction to be worked out in the best of circumstances within a marriage without trying to make one spouse responsible for the behavior of the other spouse.

The exaggeration in claims of change and cure has been documented by Jim Peron in a booklet entitled *Homosexuality and the Miracle Makers*, which makes sobering reading. He writes of many claims of change that have not stood the test of time, and he documents his statements with the names of people and the sources of his information. Peron also documents the rise and fall of various ex-gay ministries. A number of those that were active five years ago are no longer active today. Ex-gay ministries come and go. Peron notes that while in the beginning of the movement these groups were led by "ex-gays," in recent years "leadership has increasingly been placed in the hands of heterosexuals."[54]

Barbara Johnson is the mother of a gay son and author of a book, *Where Does a Mother Go to Resign?*[55] In 1977 she founded a group called SPATULA, "to bring parents down from the ceiling and the wall" when they learn a child is same-sex-oriented. While working with parents in SPATULA she has come to know many lesbian and gay persons and has become familiar with ex-gay ministries.

She talked with me about a truth that has increasingly been borne in on her during these years. She has discovered that no matter how much prayer and counseling homosexual children have received and taken part in, the percentage of those who have been able to change—and, more important, to remain changed—has been almost infinitesimal. Even those who make no pretense of becoming heterosexual but have chosen to remain celibate have found this difficult and their numbers also are small.

She has found, as Tom Minnery wrote in *Christianity Today*, that "God doesn't always respond on cue." She is critical of what she calls " 'name it and claim it' Christians who believe that to order up a cure, they need only believe hard enough."[56]

"Is it possible," she asked, during our lunch, "that God has actually created a whole segment of the population as homosexual? And if so, what can his purpose be?"

She went on to say, with some perplexity, that there did not seem to be any easy answers. She had discovered—painfully, from experience—that life does not always conform to the Bible verses we like to apply to certain situations.

Can a same-sex orientation be changed? Experience does not encourage an optimistic answer.

"Is My Child Lost for Eternity?"

Recently, the parents of a gay man came to see me. All three—father, mother, and son—are fine, intelligent, well-educated, sensitive Christians. I had met the son previously and he had asked if his parents could meet me.

After the parents and I had talked for a while, the young man's mother voiced the urgent question many Christian parents have: "If the Bible says that homosexuality is an abomination before God and that no homosexual person will inherit the kingdom of heaven, is my gay or lesbian child lost for eternity?"

If we are to be realistic, we need to recognize that the

Bible does not necessarily say what we think it says on the subject. To me, the evidence that the Bible is speaking of certain homosexual acts—which it is right in condemning—is far stronger and more believable than the idea that God condemns those who have not chosen their sexual orientation and who are unable to change. Neither can I believe that such persons are commanded to live a celibate life. Those who have included the option of celibacy in the framework of their religious lives understand that it must be a freely chosen vocation, not a forced servitude.

I believe that all persons, heterosexual and homosexual, are called by God to live sexually responsible and loving lives. Millions of married heterosexual persons are not living sexually responsible and loving lives within their marriages, as the statistics on infidelity, battering, and incest reveal. Police blotters and more formal statistical studies show that a high percentage of prostitutes' clients are married. The statistics are perhaps less accurate on the clandestine homosexual activities of married men, but gay men speak of the high percentage of married men who cruise in gay areas and pick up free homosexual sex or else hire male prostitutes. Obviously, heterosexual men and women do not always behave with impeccable morals.

I believe it is possible for lesbians and gay men to have loving, responsible, committed relationships that include genital sexual activity, and I believe that these relationships are as acceptable in God's sight as loving, responsible, committed heterosexual relationships. At present it is more difficult for gay and lesbian people to do this than for straight people, because, generally, same-sex-oriented couples receive no support for this type of relationship from either the church or society—and then we criticize them for a promiscuous life-style, which we often assume is the only type of life-style they live. In the case of gay men, not even the gay community provides much support for such a relationship. As we have seen, the lesbian community is more likely to provide support for stable, long-term lesbian relationships than does the gay male community.

In a recent book Virginia Ramey Mollenkott speaks of evaluating homosexual relationships on the basis of quality of relating rather than on the basis of the "object" with whom the relating is done. What she says is of great importance to parents of same-sex-oriented children:

Constitutional homosexual orientation is a *state of being* . . . in which the individual's most authentic and therefore deepest and holiest love-feelings flow naturally toward persons of the same rather than the other sex. To treat these love-feelings on a par with gang rape, adultery, prostitution, and acts of flagrant exploitation is to defame and deny homosexual personhood.

Concerning covenant relationships between persons of the same sex she writes: "Many church leaders persist in comparing such unions to sicknesses like alcoholism, or violations of covenant like adultery, or exploitation like bestiality. Such insensitivity fills me with rage and pain on behalf of the people whose highest love nature is being treated with contempt."[57]

The idea that sexual activity is sinful without the sanctification of marriage may be so ingrained in some parents that even a loving, caring, faithful same-sex relationship can never be acceptable to them. Or it may take them a long time to learn to live with such an arrangement for their child. If this is the case, they need to learn the truth that God does not always ratify our decisions.

Saved by Grace and by Choice

The question parents ask—"Is my gay or lesbian child lost for eternity?"—is probably emotionally the most highly charged question that could be asked. *They want to know that they will meet their child in heaven.*

The fear voiced by conservative Christians is that "sloppy agape"—love that accepts and approves of anything and everything—does not in reality help the same-sex-oriented person. They believe that if Christians do not take a tough line concerning homosexuality as sin—at least concerning homosexual acts as sin—they are encouraging actions that will exclude such a person from the kingdom of heaven and thus, in the long run, they are being cruel because they are condemning the person to eternal punishment.

I understand the cry in the heart of conservative Christians: "If we do not maintain a hard line against sin, it will engulf our world. Our churches will crumble. Our civilization will be swept away. God expects us to maintain biblical standards of righteousness." Yet surely there is a difference between compassion for persons and the condoning of every type of sin. The truth is that only love can open and unfold the human spirit.

Many conservative Christians have said, in this connection, that one should love the sinner but hate the sin. The trouble with this idea is that so often it is difficult for the "sinner" to understand the finely tuned message about whom Christians love and what they hate. And if Christians are hating a "sin" that seems to be almost an inborn condition—or at least one that the experts tell us seems to be well set by about age five—they may find themselves dealing too harshly with some of God's children.

Because I have participated in many services of lesbian and gay religious groups, I have seen at close range their need and desire for an intimate relationship with God. I wonder what would happen if churches did not discriminate against same-sex-oriented people, did not try to label them "sinners." What would happen if churches put into practice some words written by the Rev. Ann G. Suzedell?

When we read through the scriptures we cannot help but notice that divine love for the people of God as promised in the biblical narratives is not careful, not calculated, not distant. It is extravagant, risky, intimate. "When you pass through the waters, I will be with you." When you walk through fire, I will be with you. When you grieve, when you hurt, when you laugh, when you rejoice, I will be with you. "For you are honored, and precious in my sight, and I love you."[58]

The promise does not say: "I will cure everything that ails you." It says, "I will be with you, I care for you, I love you."

She goes on to quote what Henri Nouwen writes in *Out of Solitude:*

What we see, and like to see, is cure and change. But what we do not see and do not want to see is care, the participation in the pain, the solidarity in suffering, the sharing in the experience of brokenness. . . . Cure without care makes us into rulers, controllers, manipulators, and prevents a real community from taking shape. Cure without care makes us preoccupied with quick changes, impatient and unwilling to share each other's burden.[59]

Nouwen has laid his finger on the churches' dilemma in relation to homosexuality: *Heterosexual Christians want to see cure and change.* Often they do not want to participate in the pain the homosexual person experiences when he or she finally acknowledges his gayness or her lesbianism. Heterosexual Christians do not want to feel solidarity with the suffering of their lesbian sisters and gay brothers as an outcast minority. Heterosexual Christians want to cure or ostracize, but they do not want to *care*. They do not want to listen, to hear, to understand what is going on in the heart and mind and life of a gay man or a lesbian. Far easier to label such persons sinners and pass them by on the other side if they cannot meet the church's standards of change or celibacy!

No one can *know* about the afterlife in the same way we can know about this life. No one, therefore, can give you total assurance that your lesbian daughter or gay son (or for that matter you yourself) will enter heaven at the close of life here on earth. Even change to heterosexuality or celibacy cannot guarantee this for your homosexual child.

I believe a same-sex-oriented person has as much chance for salvation as anyone else. Each of us is saved by grace and by choice. Each of us is born with a spark of God's spirit within us. Some nurture this spark and learn to live in the spiritual dimension as well as in the physical. Others continue to deaden the spark until any vestige of the spiritual is either extinguished or put in the service of total evil. One's sexual orientation does not determine one's entrance into heaven; one's relationship to God does.

A fundamentalist friend who had read *My Son Eric* sat down with me to discuss the book. At one point in our conversation he said, "Mary, have you given serious thought to the fact that because of what you say in your book many gay and lesbian people will not make any effort to change and will therefore be lost?"

"Yes, Michael," I answered, "I've given the matter *very* serious thought. But have you considered that because of the church's idea about a same-sex orientation millions of lesbian and gay persons may be kept from a close relationship to God and that on Judgment Day the church may be called to account for this?"

Establishing a Relationship with God

In his book *Healing the Pain of Everyday Loss* Ira Tanner writes of a young woman who, after her husband had divorced her, prayed that God would reconcile her and her husband. Then the thought came to her that she was asking God to give her what she wanted. She realized she was not praying but begging. "She changed her prayers," Tanner says, "from begging to simply talking with God, asking him to help her through the crisis."[60]

Within your particular circumstances as the parent of a same-sex-oriented child what will you pray for? You can focus your prayers narrowly: "O God, heal my daughter (son)." Like a child, you are simply crying for what you want.

The real purpose of prayer, its real essence, is to establish and maintain a relationship and a dialogue with God, to learn the mind of the Creator, to experience redemption again and again, in each situation of our lives as it arises. What does redemption mean in this context? It means deliverance, rescue, liberation, extrication, release from a particular situation.

God has many ways of releasing us from a situation. I have often been struck by the fact that in a particular crisis I see only one way of resolving it, and if I were directing the action, I would head straight for this point. God does it so differently. God seems to have in mind another way of resolving the crisis, one that leads out into broader vistas than I, with my finite tunnel vision, could have imagined.

At this point you feel that you are in a straitjacket. Fighting the straitjacket is not going to get you out and will probably tangle things tighter. As you fight, panic rises within you, increasing your inner tension, which drives you to flail harder, which only tightens the straitjacket around you still more.

Only as you begin to relax, to be quiet, to wait, to listen, will you hear the quiet voice give instructions, a few at a time, telling you step by slow step how to exit from the straitjacket of fear and perhaps loathing in which you are trapped.

When you pray, then, say, "O God, please show me why this has happened to me, to my family. What do you want me to learn in this situation? What is the promise hidden in this event?"[61] You can add, "Thank you for the answers you are giving me." You may not have seen any answers yet, but in saying this you are indicating you do expect God to answer. You are acting out faith.

Some time ago I received a beautiful letter from the father of a gay man that illustrates so perfectly what is stated above.

I gave my heart to Jesus when I was fourteen years old. I have a lovely Christian wife, and we have three beautiful Christian children. All of them are active in the church and the community. We are Baptists and raised our children in the best Christian home we knew how to give them. We love our children, but our eldest son is our special joy. Of the three he is the most thoughtful, the most helpful, the most concerned about us. Perhaps we actually love him the most. Surely he needs our love more than the others. You see, he is gay. Living in today's world he needs all the love we can give him.

It was a shock to us when he told us, now almost three years ago, though the two younger ones had apparently known for some time. He told us one evening as we gathered for family prayers more or less in this way: "I want to tell you something, and I want you to pray for me. Don't pray for God to change me, because there can't be any change. God made me this way. Pray that God may use me even in the way He made me." And then he told us he is gay. For a few minutes we just sat in silence. Then I kneeled and began to pray aloud that God would lead us, that He would open our hearts as well as our minds to His will.

The answer did not come at once. Nor did it come easily. It came gradually and came in part through the positive Christian attitude of the younger two. We listen to our children. We discuss things with them and weigh what they have to say. We have always made it a policy never to act in haste or anger with our children. And so the answer came gradually. We observed no outward change in Peter, except that he seemed even happier than usual, if that were possible. He was always a good boy, and we realized that he is still a good boy. He is, in fact, still the same fine person he was before we knew. We soon realized that his habits had not changed. He still had the same friends. We still knew whom he went out with, where he went, and when he would come home. He was still a good influence in the church and in the community. We continued to pray for God's guidance, and eventually the answer came. We at last knew that God was saying to us, "This is your son. He is the way I made him. Love him. Love him the way he is." We know in our hearts that this is the answer God has given to us.

We told Peter by our actions that we continued to love him. Finally we told him with our words and family prayers that since God made him gay we believe that God made him that way for a purpose. My wife and I had wondered if Peter had any gay friends, but we did not want to pry into his privacy. That was another question we had to wait to have answered. One evening two of Peter's closest friends were with him at the house. When it came time for family prayers, Peter asked if they might join us. As we sat discussing what things needed to be prayed for, Peter's friends told us how happy they were that we have accepted Peter the way he is. Then Jim requested that we pray God's blessing and guidance upon his and Peter's love for each other and on their relationship. And so we prayed. Now we feel that in addition to our own fine three sons God has added two more. Truly our cup of joy runneth over. But we still pray daily that God may protect them from a hostile world and use them in His own way.

The most important words in this letter are near the middle: "The answer did not come at once. Nor did it come easily. It came gradually." The answer the letter-writer received is also important, because it is probably the beginning of your answer too: "This is your child. He (she) is the way I made him (her). Love your child. Love your child the way he (she) is."

God is waiting to open new insights, new adventures, perhaps even a whole new life to you, not despite your child's sexual orientation, but because of doors that open to you through a closer listening, a deeper relationship to God. There *is* a promise, a world of promises, hidden in this event.

Years ago—long before I learned that Eric is gay, long before my divorce—at a moment of extreme anguish, God placed in my hands a pearl of great price. I was on my way to an emergency appointment with my psychiatrist in the early days of a deep depression into which I had fallen. In my agony I cried out to God, "Why do I have to suffer so?"

And then, having discharged a small amount of my pain and desperation, I added, "If it helps somebody, sometime, it's all right."

Immediately, clearly, words were in my mind in answer to my cry: "Nothing that is given to me is ever wasted." This was the first time that God had spoken to me in such a way that I realized God was giving me a definite message. I was sure it was God speaking to me, because if I had been talking to myself, I would have said, "Nothing that is given to *God* is ever wasted."

For some reason I was comforted. The agony was still there, but it was not as sharp. The touch of deity on my life had brought a new dimension to my suffering. My pain had a purpose. We are willing to suffer if we know the suffering is not purposeless.

Then I said, "God, I give you my suffering," and I went to my appointment, having turned a significant corner in my life. Complete healing waited a long time, but I had been given a lifeline to hold on to that would pull me through many dark days ahead.

In the intervening years I have learned that the most important offering we can bring to God is not our strengths, our good points, our talents. What God wants from us is an offering of our individual pain, our weakness, the worst parts of ourselves, the worst things that happen to us. Until we offer these things God cannot begin to deal with them and transform them from loss into gain.

We never learn or grow by running away from those things within ourselves (fear, anger, temper, hatred, lust) that we do not want to admit, even to ourselves, or by running away from situations that we do not want to deal with. These things are transformed only as we summon our courage to look them in the eye, acknowledge their existence—and offer the situation to God. What God wants most of all, it would seem, is a way into the fortresses of our souls to begin the process of transformation.

Do not look for quick and easy answers. Many times this is not the way God chooses. You are starting—or perhaps continuing—on a pilgrimage. Often pilgrimages are made on foot, and hiking is not the fastest or most luxurious mode of travel. But because you proceed slowly you will learn many things along the way you would not have discovered otherwise. The goal is not to move you from here to there as quickly as possible, but to open your eyes to the beauties, the vistas, the truths, the marvelous possibilities of the land through which you travel.

Do you feel nothing good could possibly come of your daughter's lesbianism, your son's gayness? Do not keep yourself in this straitjacket. At this point in the development of the human race, change or cure for your child may not be a viable option. Open yourself to the many other possibilities God is offering you. Open the door, right where you are. One simple sentence—"God, I give you my concern over my child's sexual orientation"— will set your feet on the path.

It may be slow. Continue to pour out your thoughts and feelings to God; then wait and listen for those slight pressures on your spirit, those rare insights, the messages that may suddenly come to you as you are still and expectant before your creator. You are starting on a pilgrimage with God, and although there may be deserts and mountains to cross, do not give up. The end will be worth it.

Chapter **10**

The Goal and the Reward

The lounge was crowded with gay and lesbian persons and their parents after the Mass that begins the monthly meeting of Dignity, the national gay/lesbian Catholic organization. Every available chair was taken in the rows that had been set up. Many people were standing, and many more were sitting packed together on the floor.

This night Ellen—like me, the mother of a gay son—and I were speaking to the members of the Twin Cities chapter of Dignity and to their mothers and fathers about the interaction between parents and same-sex-oriented children when the children come out to their parents. We made our presentations, and then the meeting was opened for discussion and questions. A brisk exchange went on for some time.

Then a mother stood up and began to tell what had happened to her on Mother's Day, a week or two before. Her account went something like this:

For a long time Thomas has been wanting me to meet some of his friends. I told him, "I accept you. I love you just as much as I did before, but I want no part of your gay life, I don't want to meet your gay friends, and if you have a lover don't tell me about it."

This past Mother's Day I had one of the most beautiful Mother's Days anyone could have. My son had wanted to take me to the Sheraton-Ritz, but the workers there were on strike, and he told me instead that one of his friends had invited me to his home for brunch.

I'm happy that I went. I loved each and every one of them. They're beautiful people! I was ashamed of the feelings that I'd had. And I'm sorry to say this to the heterosexual world, but I saw more love in this church tonight than I've seen in a long time.

You should have heard the applause as she finished! A lot of eyes were damp too.

I do not remember what Ellen and I said that evening; I do not remember any of the discussion or questions. But several years later I remember clearly what that mother said. Her spontaneous account of an important turning point in her relationship with her son summed up the purpose of the meeting. She was a living demonstration that even parents who are in their sixties and seventies *can* readjust their thinking. The satisfaction and joy she radiated because of the change in her thinking made a powerful impact on the whole gathering.

Ellen, who shared the program with me that night, is another parent who has discovered a new dimension to life because of her gay son. I had not known her before she learned about her son's sexual orientation. When I met her I met a vital, concerned, outgoing woman. She has since told me she used to be quiet and retiring. Sometimes the hard experiences of life do cause the opening and flowering of unsuspected characteristics and talents.

I think of another mother who, two years ago, was devastated to learn that her son is gay. Today she, her son, and his lover share a home. This *can* happen. This *does* happen. Why should this not happen?

We cannot afford to lose even one of our children. If death comes, we have to accept it. We can do nothing else. But to shut the door on a child because she or he does not fit our expectations is a double cruelty—to us and to the child.

"I feel terrible sadness and pathos over the beautiful 'children' many parents are missing because sexuality gets in the way," writes Peggy Way, a United Church of Christ minister who has counseled many lesbian and gay persons. "All the rich humanness, spirituality, commitment, kindness I get to enjoy and share is lost to parents who cannot deal with the homosexuality of their own children, regardless of their other fine qualities."[1]

I believe the effort to cope with the information that your child is lesbian or gay is worthwhile, as is the investment of a considerable amount of time and perhaps even a good deal of money as you come to terms with your child's sexual orientation. To do this may take courage. To accomplish this may be painful and almost certainly will require hard work and determination on your part as you learn about a same-sex orientation, meet your child's lover, meet some of his or her other friends.

Is it worth all this? A thousand times yes! This is, as Robert Browning said in a different context, "the last of life for which the first was made."[2] Do not cheat yourself of the years when you can enjoy your grown-up children. Do not cheat yourself of what Joan Mills has called "the best part of parenting; the final, firmest bonding; the goal and the reward."[3] There is no reason why, simply because one of your children happens to be same-sex- rather than other-sex-oriented, you should miss out on your reward.

Don't let denial of your very real feelings of grief rob you of what is rightfully yours.

Judy Tatelbaum writes:

Grief is a wound that needs attention in order to heal. To work through and complete grief means to face our feelings openly and honestly, to express or release our feelings fully, and to tolerate and accept our feelings for however long it takes for the wound to heal. . . . The only grief that does not end is grief that has not been fully faced.[4]

Use all the resources that are available to you—those mentioned at intervals throughout this book and those you may discover for yourself.

In the prologue to her book, Tatelbaum quotes from *The Prophet*, by Kahlil Gibran: "Your joy is your sorrow unmasked. And the selfsame well from which your laughter rises was oftentimes filled with your tears."[5]

It is these experiences that threaten to destroy us which can also open us up to the most intense experiences of growth and ultimate joy. I want to emphasize that word ultimate. Because growth can be painful, sometimes we try to avoid it. Joy comes only after we have submitted to the growth.

Any experience that wounds has the potential for cracking open the tight, constricting husk that often imprisons a part or all of one's soul. Confronting your child's same-sex orientation is one of these experiences. You will not escape the confrontation without pain. Your only choice is whether the pain is going to be destructive to you, to your enjoyment of life, and to your relationship with your child, or whether you are going to allow the pain to be a constructive influence in your life. Are you going to allow it to open you up? Are you going to allow yourself to grow? Are you going to come to grips with this unwelcome circumstance and make it into something that broadens and deepens your life?

None of us wants to experience the destruction of his or

her hopes, dreams, goals. It seems to us that a dark cloud has descended on us, obliterating the familiar landscape about us. Before us stands a bleak, forbidding door that promises us nothing but separation from everything we had hoped for. We can choose to remain outside this door for the rest of our lives, but we cannot go back to life as it was before. We can also, by our own volition, step through the doorway. Probably the majority of parents of same-sex-oriented children are dragged, protesting, through the doorway into what may seem to us to be the utter void on the other side.

"There was no strain of music from within, no smell of eternal orchards at the threshold," C.S. Lewis wrote about his experience of being "dragged through the doorway" as his atheism yielded reluctantly to faith.[6] Each of us at some time in life is dragged through a doorway he or she would not have chosen. We see only what we believe is the everlasting extinction of our dreams. We cannot imagine that there will ever again be music or fruitful orchards in our lives.

There can be joy on the other side of bleakness, of darkness. How could I have known that out of divorce and then out of learning of my son's gayness would come some of the most fulfilling experiences of my life?

It *can* happen. There is no reason why it should not.

One final recommendation is important: Start now! For a time denial may be necessary for you to survive. Do not make it a way of life.

Begin to take hold of the circumstance that has befallen you. Act now. None of us knows what time allotment she or he may still have in which to accomplish this reconciliation of her or his feelings. Judy Tatelbaum, a much younger woman than I, writes: "Time is passing quickly. . . . At twenty I disliked the sense that life felt endless, and I liked the idea that I had plenty of time. Now I no longer feel that I have plenty of time. I want to act now, before it is too late."[7]

Further on she writes: "Frequently after a loss I have heard people say something like 'Never again will I hide my love from my family and friends.'" We bring great sorrow on ourselves when we have to live with unexpressed feelings of love after the death of a loved one. It is, Tatelbaum says, a painful lesson that many people have to learn.[8]

You do not have to learn this lesson. You can decide not to withhold your love from your child. Approval is not the same as love. You do not need to approve of *everything* your child does in order to love him or her. Surely you do not approve of *everything* your heterosexual children do.

Do not withdraw from your emotions: your anger at your child, at yourself—yes, even perhaps at God; your feelings of guilt; your fear of pain and of the unknown; your anger at your vulnerability and your fear of this vulnerability. Most important, do not withdraw from your love. The person you hurt most by withholding love is yourself. Yes, you *do* hurt your child, but of even more significance is the fact that you shrink and wither yourself. The floodgates that shut off or release pain are the same floodgates that shut off or release all emotions, including love. You cannot shut off pain or anger without also shutting off love.

Let yourself hurt; let yourself weep; let yourself be angry; let yourself love; let yourself live. Life is too short to waste in the chill, gray winter of blighted hopes and chosen separation from a loved one. No one else can end this winter for you. You have to make the effort yourself.

A new chapter of your life awaits you. It may even contain music and fruitful orchards. It can still bring you the rewards of parenting—the final, firmest bonding of adult parent to adult child, the goal and reward for which you gave up many of your own desires, worked, walked the floor nights, hauled carfuls of squealing youngsters, attended PTA meetings and Little League games, and sat through such milestone ceremonies as graduation.

Your daughter, your son, is reaching out to you, wanting to maintain a real, loving, caring relationship with you. Your child has shared with you a part of her or his life that is significant to her or him. Therefore you can rejoice. Your child is alive. Your child is reaching out to you in love. Accept this love and give back yours.

Rejoice—and enjoy your child!

Appendix 1

Coming-out Letter from Rick to His Family

New York City
December 20, 1978

Dear Family,

Merry Christmas. I hope this note finds you all in good health and humor.

You have not heard much of me, and unless you've been reading between the lines, you know even less of the story of my last year. I hope to give all of you autographed hardcover editions when I can settle down to write it; but at this point I have only the energy to give a summary of what it feels like to be me as I stand at the summit of 1978 and look out over the prospect of 1979.

As for my '78: My list of acquisitions does not include a bank account of any great weight; but I do own a beautiful oriental rug, a desk, several tables and chairs, many books, and a considerable (though used) wardrobe. I also have a decent job and a habitable one-bedroom apartment at reasonable rent in a fair neighborhood. But my most prized possession at this moment is one purchased only in small part by money; that is, my survival. As I survey my wealth, I am not displeased.

My calculation of my image is more difficult. In the eyes of those who truly know me, I feel it has been enhanced in 1978; they have told me as much. However, among many who would, or feel they should, know me—but do not—my image is unclear. This is due, in part, to a conscious decision on my part a year ago to restrict information based on which family, friends, and acquaintances could alter their impressions. I went through some wrenching changes and didn't want to have to explain or justify myself as I was doing it.

A year ago I left Arizona, where I was involved in, among other things, a very intense loving relationship with Karla.* She is an open, honest, intelligent, and sensitive human being, and I loved her as a lover and an ally, and I loved her son in a way as close to parental as our relative proximity in ages and our newness to each other would allow. I was, in a way and to an extent previously inconceivable, happy.

Her love did everything I'd always hoped a love would do . . . almost. The only disappointment was that her love did not overwhelm or subsume my sexual and emotional attraction to men.

There. I said it.

For some reason, I'd always assumed that the love of the Right Woman would "mature" me out of my "aberrant" feelings and so had never experienced relating to men other than in rather narrowly defined ways—ways acceptable to our homophobic society. When, after a year of various degrees of intimacy with Karla—most of it wonderful, all of it satisfactory—I still found my eye wandering and my heart wondering, I could lie to her no longer. Nor could I lie to myself. So I told her then what I am telling you now. And I left her and pursued the only thing I really know: that is, how I feel.

It's been a long year, easier in many ways than most years because of the relative lack of dissimulation I've felt I had to put out; but difficult in the intensity of the overhaul (emotional, spiritual, interpersonal, etc.) I've subjected myself to. It's been worth it: I feel much closer on the track toward a view of life and love and my role with others than I did a year ago. I have honest relationships based on affection and respect with both men and women. I hope to find a life/love partner with whom to share the years, and at this point I feel I would prefer a man. This may not always be so, but my attraction to men goes back at least seventeen years, and I have never been particularly attracted to women, at least not physically. (Although I must say that emotionally I find more women more compatible than most men.) It's possible that I may not find a partner in any traditional sense, and so I am striving for the strength to face life autonomously or in nontraditional relationships.

*Name changed

Since I have few expectations, I have less than most to fear from loneliness.

My image? Whether it be enhanced or diminished in the eyes of any particular person is of less concern to me than this: I have never felt clearer, more honest, more self-directed, and more confident . . . in my life.

So, my memories of 1978? They are too many, too complex, too extreme, and too personal to recount here. But I'll tell anybody anything they're willing to hear with an open mind. I love you all and would like to know you. I welcome you to know and love me.

1979? There is much work for me to do, and a changed, freer person goes about the tasks. I have sifted through a couple hundred pounds of seven years of writings, correspondences, and memorabilia over the past week or two, and I think some of the writings are in near-publishable form. My intention is to polish and try to sell some lyrics and short stories. The specific time and space plans haven't gelled yet.

So. That's the main of what's new in my life, and I want to end this before I decide not to send it. The time for these things never seems right; but today I feel strong and have faith in your love.

All my love, and a hope that 1979 brings to you the peace and hope I have found this past year.

Rick

Note: For the sake of brevity several parts of the letter have been deleted. All that pertains to Rick's coming out to his family has been retained in his own words.

Appendix 2

Resources

Parents and Friends of Lesbians and Gays

One of the most helpful organizations that you, as a parent, could become involved with at this time in your life is a Parents and Friends of Lesbians and Gays group. To find out if there is such a group near you, write to:

> Parents FLAG
> P.O. Box 24565
> Los Angeles, CA 90024
> Phone: (213) 472-8952

Enclose a long (#10), stamped, self-addressed envelope.

Listing of Lesbian and Gay Religious Groups

For a listing of the national headquarters of various same-sex-oriented religious groups, such as Integrity (Episcopal), Dignity (Catholic), Lutherans Concerned, Presbyterians for Lesbian and Gay Concerns, and Universal Fellowship of Metropolitan Community churches, write to me:

> Mary V. Borhek
> P.O. Box 13331
> St. Paul, MN 55113

Enclose a long (#10), stamped, self-addressed envelope and an extra first-class stamp to cover cost of printing and handling.

Notes

Introduction: A Two-way Mirror

1. Alan P. Bell, et al., *Sexual Preference* (Bloomington, IN: Indiana University Press, 1981), p. 222.

Chapter 1: So You Want to Come Out to Your Parents

1. M. Scott Peck, *The Road Less Traveled* (New York: Simon & Schuster, 1979), pp. 131, 16.

Chapter 2: The Big Decision

1. Mary V. Borhek, *My Son Eric* (New York: The Pilgrim Press, 1979).
2. Augustus Y. Napier, with Carl A. Whitaker, *The Family Crucible* (New York: Bantam Books, 1980), p. 208.
3. Don Clark, *Loving Someone Gay* (Millbrae, CA: Celestial Arts, 1977), p. 68.
4. Napier, *The Family Crucible,* op. cit.

Chapter 3: Grief Often Does Not Look Like Grief

1. Peter Marris, *Loss and Change* (Garden City, NY: Anchor Press/Doubleday, 1975), p. 9.
2. Ira J. Tanner, *Healing the Pain of Everyday Loss* (Minneapolis: Winston Press, 1976), pp. 54–55.
3. Judith Guest, *Ordinary People* (New York: Ballantine Books, 1977).

Chapter 4: Getting Ready to Make the Big Announcement

1. Ira J. Tanner, *Healing the Pain of Everyday Loss* (Minneapolis: Winston Press, 1976), p. 24.
2. Clinton R. Jones, *Understanding Gay Relatives and Friends* (New York: Seabury Press, 1978).
3. Judith Guest, *Ordinary People* (New York: Ballantine Books, 1977).
4. Theodore Isaac Rubin, *The Angry Book* (New York: Collier Books/Macmillan, 1969).

Chapter 5: Working Through Grief—Together

1. Letha Scanzoni and Virginia Ramey Mollenkott, *Is the Homosexual My Neighbor?* (New York: Harper & Row, 1978), pp. 32–34.
2. Lawrence J. Hatterer, *Changing Homosexuality in the Male* (New York: McGraw-Hill, 1970), and Donahue Transcript #10141, with Phil Donahue, Alan Bell, and Lawrence Hatterer, p. 32; available from Multimedia Program Productions, P.O. Box 2111, Cincinnati, OH 45201.
3. Aesthetic realism is a philosophy founded by Eli Siegel and taught by him and others since the early 1940s. It explains the cause of homosexuality thus: "(1) All homosexuality arises from contempt of the world, not liking it sufficiently. (2) This changes into a contempt for women." A fuller explanation is contained in the book *The H Persuasion* (New York: Definition Press).
4. See Betty Fairchild and Nancy Hayward, *Now That You Know* (New York: Harcourt Brace Jovanovich, 1979), pp. 77–81, for an explanation of the Kinsey scale.
5. William H. Masters and Virginia E. Johnson, *Homosexuality in Perspective* (Boston: Little, Brown & Co., 1979). The Lutheran Campus Ministry study group referred to earlier had this to say concerning the book: "(a) Masters and Johnson report a treatment failure rate (note carefully the term!) of 28.4 per cent in their treatment of 54 males and 13 females who expressed *dissatisfaction* with their homosexuality. (b) Masters and Johnson do not treat homosexuality, which they consider a natural sexual expression. They treat only the sexual dysfunction or dissatisfaction of those who want to *convert* (Kinsey's 5s and 6s) or

revert (Kinsey's 2s, 3s, and 4s) to heterosexual expressions. The key component in their therapy is a rigorous neutrality on the part of the therapists. (c) The results of the Masters and Johnson study are not easily generalized beyond their mode of treatment. They are highly selective of their subjects and refuse those who come to them under opprobrium of the court or threat of job loss. Those selected must be highly motivated and willing to spend two weeks in St. Louis in a sophisticated program with a very competent staff. (d) The Masters and Johnson treatment is an *in vivo* modification of the erotic response system of an individual with a supportive partner. Thus they present a new approach to the treatment of sexual dysfunction and dissatisfaction."

6. In "Homosexuality and the Miracle-Makers" Jim Peron writes: "To the vast majority of people 'ex-gay' would seem to mean someone who no longer has homosexual desires and is reoriented towards heterosexuality. But to Exodus [an ex-gay organization] the word has a different meaning. . . . One tape produced by Love in Action, an affiliate of Exodus, in San Rafael, CA, specifically states that an 'ex-gay' is only a homosexual who has turned his life over to Jesus Christ and been 'born-again,' it does not mean someone who has been reoriented sexually" (p. 2). Available from Free Forum Books, Box 242, West Willington, CT 06279.

7. Alan P. Bell, et al., *Sexual Preference* (Bloomington, IN: Indiana University Press, 1981).

8. Ibid., p. 222.

9. Victor Paul Furnish, *The Moral Teaching of Paul* (Nashville: Abingdon Press, 1979), pp. 62–63.

10. Erving Goffman's book, *Stigma* (Englewood Cliffs, NJ: Prentice-Hall, 1963), examines in detail the reaction of all stigmatized persons and the strategies they employ in dealing with the refusal of others to accept them on the same basis as everyone else.

Chapter 6: The Other Side

1. *Minneapolis Tribune*, April 9, 1978.
2. *Minneapolis Star, Saturday*, November 12, 1977.

3. No inference should be taken from this that any child who is not getting along well with his or her peers is same-sex-oriented. There are many reasons for a child's difficulties in relationships with others. Similarly, it is normal for children to "hang around" with other children of the same sex. Either of these behaviors can be indicative of other difficulties—or nothing more than usual developmental patterns.

4. Del Martin and Phyllis Lyon, *Lesbian/Woman* (New York: Bantam Books, 1972).

5. *Minneapolis Tribune,* April 20, 1978.

6. Paul H. Moore, Jr., *Take a Bishop Like Me* (New York: Harper & Row, 1979), p. 75.

Chapter 7: Letting Go

1. *St. Paul Dispatch,* December 5, 1979.

2. Florida Scott-Maxwell, *The Measure of My Days* (New York: Knopf, 1968), pp. 16–17.

3. Erich Fromm, *The Art of Loving* (New York: Harper & Row, 1956), pp. 42–43 (italics added).

4. Ibid., pp. 36–37.

5. Thomas A. Harris, *I'm OK—You're OK* (New York: Harper & Row, 1969), clarifies the concepts of parent, child, and adult and gives an insight into the ways in which we all relate to other people out of these three modes.

6. Scott-Maxwell, *The Measure of My Days,* op. cit., p. 16.

7. Fromm, *The Art of Loving,* op. cit., p. 17.

8. Judy Tatelbaum, *The Courage to Grieve* (New York: Harper & Row, 1980).

Chapter 8: Parents Also Come Out

1. Carl Whitaker, in Augustus Y. Napier, *The Family Crucible,* (New York: Bantam Books, 1980), p. 253.

Chapter 9: Religious Issues and a Same-sex Orientation

1. John Boswell, *Christianity, Social Tolerance, and Homosexuality* (Chicago: University of Chicago Press, 1980), p. 335.

2. Francis Schaeffer, *No Final Conflict* (Downers Grove, IL: InterVarsity Press, 1976), p. 16.

3. John Marsh, *The Gospel of St. John* (New York: Penguin Books, 1979), pp. 48ff.

4. Clyde S. Kilby, *The Christian World of C.S. Lewis* (Grand Rapids, MI: Eerdmans, 1964), pp. 153–54.

5. Richard and Catherine Clark Kroeger, "Pandemonium and Silence at Corinth," *The Reformed Journal*, June 1978.

6. Virginia Ramey Mollenkott, *Speech, Silence, Action!* (Nashville: Abingdon Press, 1980), p. 135.

7. See James Strong, *The Exhaustive Concordance of the Bible* (Nashville: Abingdon Press, 1973 edition).

8. Boswell, *Christianity, Social Tolerance, and Homosexuality,* op. cit., p. 100. Leviticus 11:7 prohibits eating of pork; Leviticus 15:24, intercourse during menstruation.

9. Ibid.

10. Strong, *The Exhaustive Concordance of the Bible,* op. cit.

11. Victor Paul Furnish, *The Moral Teaching of Paul* (Nashville: Abingdon Press, 1979), pp. 73–78.

12. Richard Lovelace, *Homosexuality and the Church* (Old Tappan, NJ: Fleming H. Revell Co., 1978), p. 93.

13. Ibid., p. 94 (italics added).

14. Charles W. Keysor, ed., *What You Should Know About Homosexuality* (Grand Rapids, MI: Zondervan, 1979), p. 26.

15. Morton T. Kelsey, *God, Dreams and Revelation* (Minneapolis: Augsburg, 1974), p. 198.

16. Keysor, *What You Should Know,* op. cit., p. 30.

17. Ibid., pp. 36–37.

18. Ibid., p. 37.

19. Ibid., p. 75.

20. Boswell, *Christianity, Social Tolerance, and Homosexuality,* op. cit., pp. 106–07. The two Greek words Boswell is speaking of are *malakoi* and *arsenokoitai.*

21. Furnish, *The Moral Teaching of Paul,* op. cit., pp. 57–58.

22. The Rev. John J. McNeill, S.J., is a Jesuit priest, a moral theologian, and author of *The Church and the Homosexual* (New York: Pocket Books, Inc., 1978).

23. Donald Goergen, *The Sexual Celibate* (New York: Seabury Press, 1974), pp. 2–3.

24. James B. Nelson, *Embodiment* (Minneapolis: Augsburg, 1978), pp. 198–99.

25. Tim LaHaye, *The Unhappy Gays* (Wheaton, IL: Tyndale House Publishers, 1978), p. 62.

26. John Money and Patricia Tucker, *Sexual Signatures* (Boston: Little, Brown & Co., 1975), pp. 37–38.

27. Ibid., p. 78.

28. Ibid., p. 24.

29. LaHaye, *The Unhappy Gays*, op. cit., pp. 65–85.

30. Irving Bieber, et al., *Homosexuality* (New York: Basic Books, 1962).

31. LaHaye, *The Unhappy Gays*, op. cit., p. 44.

32. Ibid., pp. 52–53.

33. Ibid., p. 49.

34. Ibid., pp. 46, 71, 75–76.

35. Ibid., p. 88.

36. Ibid., p. 190.

37. Ibid., p. 202.

38. Greg L. Bahnsen, *Homosexuality: A Biblical View* (Grand Rapids, MI: Baker Book House, 1978), p. 127.

39. Frank DuMas, *Gay Is Not Good* (Nashville: Thomas Nelson, Inc., 1979).

40. Lovelace, *Homosexuality and the Church*, op. cit., p. 91.

41. Keysor, *What You Should Know*, op. cit., p. 54.

42. Furnish, *The Moral Teaching of Paul*, op. cit., p. 63.

43. Ibid., p. 65.

44. Kenneth O. Gangel, *The Gospel and the Gay* (Nashville: Thomas Nelson, Inc., 1978), p. 164.

45. Ibid., p. 165.

46. Jerry Kirk, *The Homosexual Crisis in the Mainline Church* (Nashville: Thomas Nelson, Inc., 1978), p. 115.

47. Ibid., pp. 89–90. The therapists Kirk is referring to are Robert R. Carkhuff; James Mallory, M.D.; and Robert Neuremberger, Ph.D.

48. Keysor, *What You Should Know*, op. cit., p. 167.

49. Ibid., p. 210.

50. Money and Tucker, *Sexual Signatures*, op. cit., pp. 165–66.

51. C.S. Lewis, *The World's Last Night* (New York: Harcourt Brace Jovanovich, 1960), pp. 4–5.

52. Arno Karlen, *Sexuality and Homosexuality* (New York: W.W. Norton & Co., 1971), p. 440.

53. Tom Minnery, "Homosexuals *Can* Change," *Christianity Today,* February 6, 1981, p. 38.

54. See note 6, chapter 5. A fuller treatment of this matter was made by Dr. Ralph Blair, of Evangelicals Concerned (30 East 60th Street, New York, NY 10022), in "The 'Ex-Gay' Movement: A Critical Analysis," a paper he presented at the annual convention of the Christian Association for Psychological Studies, April 1982, Atlanta, GA.

55. Barbara Johnson, *Where Does a Mother Go to Resign?* (Minneapolis: Bethany Fellowship, Inc., 1979). The naming of SPATULA is referred to on p. 144.

56. Minnery, "Homosexuals *Can* Change," *Christianity Today,* op. cit., p. 39.

57. Virginia Ramey Mollenkott, *Speech, Silence, Action!* (Nashville: Abingdon Press, 1980), pp. 133–34.

58. Ann G. Suzedell, *Accent,* April 1981, Vol. 10, No. 2, published by Moravian Theological Seminary, Bethlehem, PA. The Bible passage she refers to and quotes is Isaiah 43:2, 4.

59. Henri Nouwen, *Out of Solitude* (Notre Dame, IN: Ave Maria Press, 1980), pp. 32, 36.

60. Ira J. Tanner, *Healing the Pain of Everyday Loss* (Minneapolis: Winston Press, 1976), p. 167.

61. Nouwen, *Out of Solitude,* op. cit., p. 57.

Chapter 10: The Goal and the Reward

1. Peggy Way, "Homosexual Counseling as a Learning Ministry," *Christianity and Crisis,* Vol. 37, Nos. 9 and 10 (May 30 and June 13, 1977), p. 128.

2. From Robert Browning, "Rabbi Ben Ezra."

3. Joan Mills, "Season of the Empty Nest," *Reader's Digest,* January 1981, p. 118.

4. Judy Tatelbaum, *The Courage to Grieve* (New York: Harper & Row, 1980), p. 9.

5. Kahlil Gibran, *The Prophet* (New York: Alfred A. Knopf, 1978), p. 32.

6. C.S. Lewis, *Surprised by Joy* (New York: Harcourt Brace Jovanovich, 1955), pp. 230–31.

7. Tatelbaum, *The Courage to Grieve,* op. cit., p. 4.

8. Ibid., p. 133.

For Further Reading

To list all the books available to help parents gain information and come to terms with a child's same-sex orientation would be impossible. The books included here have been helpful to me, but they are by no means the only ones. They represent at least a point of departure for a parent's pilgrimage. Some of these books also have listings for further reading. In addition, possibly the books, pamphlets, and articles cited in the Notes might catch the reader's interest.

Coming to an understanding of a child's same-sex orientation is not the only goal of this book. The deepening of understanding and relationships within the whole family is another important objective. For this reason I have listed a number of books that, in many cases, do not mention a same-sex orientation but that might help to increase harmony within the family group.

For those who are having difficulties with a same-sex orientation because of religious views, I have included a number of books that take a positive view.

Books About Grief

Lester, Andrew D. *It Hurts So Bad, Lord!* Nashville: Broadman Press, 1976. Chapters 1 and 2, dealing with the crisis of depression and the recovery of hope, are particularly pertinent for parents.

Miller, William A. *When Going to Pieces Holds You Together.* Minneapolis: Augsburg Publishing House, 1976. Readable book with good insights into the grieving process.

Tanner, Ira J. *Healing the Pain of Everyday Loss.* Minneapolis: Winston Press, 1980. More than most authors who write books on grief, Tanner discusses grief resulting not only from death, but from many relatively ordinary occurrences.

Tatelbaum, Judy. *The Courage to Grieve.* New York: Harper & Row, Publishers, 1980. Although this book deals mainly with grief resulting from death, it includes a wealth of material that can be translated to the process of grieving over one's child's sexual orientation.

John E. Fortunato's book, *Embracing the Exile,* listed below with the religious books, contains several chapters organized around the subject of grief.

Information for Parents About a Same-sex Orientation

Borhek, Mary V. *My Son Eric.* New York: The Pilgrim Press, 1979. How the author found out she has a gay son and the process she went through as her strongly anti-homosexual stand evolved into acceptance and positive action.

Fairchild, Betty, and Nancy Hayward. *Now That You Know.* New York: Harcourt Brace Jovanovich, 1981. A general, comprehensive book about same-sex orientation, written by parents for parents. Includes many parents' experiences.

Hobson, Laura Z. *Consenting Adult.* New York: Warner Books, 1976. A novel about a mother coming to terms with her son's same-sex orientation, written by a woman who faced the same situation.

Jones, Clinton R. *Understanding Gay Relatives and Friends.* New York: The Seabury Press, 1978. Just what the title indicates—a book to help involved persons gain insight into a same-sex orientation, written by a caring and experienced counselor who is an Episcopal priest.

Money, John, and Patricia Tucker. *Sexual Signatures.* Boston: Little, Brown & Co., 1975. A basic look at why people are male or female, same- or other-sex-oriented, written in a nontechnical, nonthreatening way.

Scanzoni, Letha, and Virginia Ramey Mollenkott. *Is the Homosexual My Neighbor?* New York: Harper & Row, Publishers, 1980. Although written from a positive Christian perspective, this book contains such a wealth of information about the whole matter of a same-sex orientation—stigma, stereotyping, science, homophobia, etc,—that it is helpful to anyone.

Silverstein, Charles. *A Family Matter: A Parent's Guide to Homosexuality*. New York: McGraw-Hill Book Co., 1978. Information for parents about a same-sex orientation, ways in which families can talk together about it, and an informative section on "Society, Medicine and Homosexuality," in which the matter of "cure" is examined from a medical point of view.

Switzer, David K., and Shirley Switzer. *Parents of the Homosexual*. Philadelphia: The Westminster Press, 1980. Deals not only with moral and religious aspects of a same-sex orientation from a positive standpoint, but also family—parent and child—relationships and the feelings of guilt parents so often feel.

Books Dealing with Understanding One's Self and Creating Better Family Relationships

Harris, Thomas A. *I'm OK—You're OK*. New York: Harper & Row, Publishers, 1969. Particularly good in explaining the specialized meanings of parent/adult/child as one means of understanding our interaction with others, especially our own parents or our own children.

Lenz, Elinor. *Once My Child, Now My Friend*. New York: Warner Books, 1981. A guide for parents in learning to become friends with adult children and put aside the former guide, mentor, and authority role suitable to younger children.

Lieberman, Mendel, and Marion Hardie. *Resolving Family Conflicts: Everybody Wins*. Santa Cruz, CA: Orenda-Unity Press. A much fuller exposition of methods suggested in chapter 6, "Getting Ready to Make the Big Announcement"; also helpful for parents who want to "hear" what their spouses and children—straight or gay—are saying.

Miller, Sherrod, et al. *Straight Talk*. New York: Rawson, Wade Publishers, 1980. Helpful in making one aware of why one's communication with another often misfires, along with help in changing methods of communication to avoid unproductive, damaging exchanges and substitute helpful, constructive dialogue.

Napier, Augustus Y., with Carl A. Whitaker. *The Family Crucible*. New York: Bantam Books, 1980. A readable, nontechnical book that can provide insights into why families behave as they do.

Peck, M. Scott. *The Road Less Traveled*. New York: Simon & Schuster, 1978. A book for both parents and children, with basic information about love, traditional values, and spiritual growth. Although written in a heterosexual context, Peck's analysis of love can also be illuminating to same-sex-oriented people.

Rubin, Theodore Isaac. *The Angry Book*. New York: Collier Books/Macmillan, 1970. Easily readable examination of the devious and unrecognized ways that anger shows up in our lives.

Sanford, John A. *Between People*. New York: Paulist Press, 1982. A book about communication one-to-one. Not a substitute for *Resolving Family Conflicts*, but with insights of its own and a somewhat more psychological orientation.

Satir, Virginia. *Peoplemaking*. Palo Alto, CA: Science and Behavior Books, 1972. A good-humored, easily understood book about the nitty-gritty of family life that can provide insights even for those whose families are grown or for children no longer in the nest.

Books and Articles with a Positive Religious View

In addition to *Is the Homosexual My Neighbor?* and *Parents of the Homosexual*, listed under the information heading above, the following publications present information and viewpoints worth thinking about from a religious point of view.

Anon. "Must Homosexuals Be Jewish Outcasts?" from *Sh'ma*, Vol. 5, No. 98 (October 3, 1978), pp. 303–5. Reprinted in *Homosexuality and Ethics*, edited by Edward Batchelor Jr. New York: The Pilgrim Press, 1980. What it is like to be a Jewish homosexual person.

Boswell, John. *Christianity, Social Tolerance, and Homosexuality*. Chicago: University of Chicago Press, 1980. A minutely detailed analysis of scriptural references commonly supposed to deal with homosexual acts is found in chapter 4, "The Scriptures," and Appendix 1, "Lexicography and St. Paul."

Fortunato, John E. *Embracing the Exile: Healing Journeys of Gay Christians*. New York: The Seabury Press, 1982. The author's riveting personal story, three chapters dealing with grief (one of them "Grieving Gay") and an invitation to heterosexual and homosexual persons alike to grow and deepen spiritually through the hard experiences of life. Note: The "healing" referred to in the subtitle has nothing to do with cure or change.

Furnish, Victor Paul. *The Moral Teaching of Paul*. Nashville: Abingdon Press, 1979. Chapter 3, "Homosexuality," while far less detailed than Boswell's material, is nevertheless well supported and scholarly without sacrificing readability by the average person.

Gittelsohn, Roland. *Love, Sex and Marriage: A Jewish View*. New York: Union of American Hebrew Congregations, 1980. One of not too many Jewish books that deal with homosexuality in a positive way, although the section is small—pp. 168–70.

Matt, Hershel. "Sin, Crime, Sickness or Alternative Life Style: A Jewish Approach to Homosexuality," *Judaism*, Vol. 27, No. 1, (Winter 1978), pp. 13–24. Reprinted in *Homosexuality and Ethics*, edited by Edward Batchelor Jr. New York: The Pilgrim Press, 1980. A thorough-going examination of the theology of homosexuality in light of the teachings of the Torah. Essentially a positive viewpoint.

McNeill, John J. *The Church and the Homosexual*. New York: Pocket Books, 1978. While the whole book deals with material of a religious nature, parents may find chapter 2, "Scripture and Homosexuality," most pertinent to their interests. Especially good for Catholics.

Mollenkott, Virginia Ramey. *Speech, Silence, Action!* Nashville: Abingdon Press, 1980. Chapter 13, "The Divine Worth of Gay Persons," is brief but contains some important and helpful insights.

Nelson, James B. *Embodiment*. Minneapolis: Augsburg Publishing House, 1979. Chapter 8, "Gayness and Homosexuality: Issues for the Church," deals with biblical interpretation, attitudes of the church toward homosexuality, a look at reasons why homosexuality is disturbing to many people, and implications for the church in ministering to same-sex-oriented persons.

Pennington, Sylvia. *But Lord, They're Gay*. Published by Lambda Christian Fellowship, P.O. Box 1967, Hawthorne, CA 90250, $5.00 plus $1.00 postage. The author's story of how God took her from "saving homosexuals" by trying to change them, to ministry to a lesbian/gay congregation. Especially good for those with evangelical and fundamentalist attitudes.

Pittenger, W. Norman. *Making Sexuality Human*. New York: The Pilgrim Press, 1979. Chapter 6, "The Homosexual Expression of Sexuality," deals with Christian ethical concepts of sexuality as they relate to same-sex-orientation. The entire book relates sexuality in all its aspects to Christian ethics in a readable way.